Now we're talking.

Now we're talking.

By Harry H Poggins

Published by CreateSpace

NOW WE'RE TALKING

ISBN 978-1-519-77478-1

Contents

If you thought melons, shopping trolleys, teapots, trainers, doorknobs, taps, cookers, schoolbags, biros, plugs and pebbles couldn't talk, think again.

They're just some of the characters in this book, and they're quite a lot like people – bonkers without knowing they are.

When they asked me to write about them, they wanted me to call the book 'Jim and the talking, marble, shopping trolley, teapot, potato, robot, shark, trainers, seashell, bench, sign, sailboat, catch, spider, schoolbag, plug, gherkin, crow, flip-flop, pants, watch, stethoscope...and so on. Bonkers! They just didn't understand there was no way I could fit all that on the cover. (To a talking schoolbag anything's possible.) Finally they agreed on 'Now we're talking' as a title.

It's a true story of course – all except the bit about a tame toilet roll. (It was actually semi-wild.) +HP

1
Poo!

When Jim opened his eyes, the first thing he saw was an enormous brown lizard, or maybe an African bull elephant that had been wallowing in mud. Strange that it should be wearing sunglasses and a small red bathing suit. Stranger still, it was holding a glass with a tiny pink umbrella poking out from it.

On closer inspection it turned out to be a photo of Jim's mega-overweight auntie Doreen holidaying on the Costa del Slob. (Where she'd been chased by enthusiastic whale watchers while swimming in the sea.)

Jim's mum had brought the photo into his bedroom to show him what a good time his auntie was having, and to get Jim up for school.

"Doreen's always going away somewhere nice," his mum said, opening his bedroom curtains. Unfortunately she'd made the mistake of putting his auntie's photo on Jim's bedside table next to the mad marble, the unreliable robot and dopey Mister Potato Head, who were all looking at it and giggling.

"Jim's auntie Doreen's so fat, she caused a tsunami when she dived in the sea," the marble whispered to the robot. "It almost capsized three car ferries!"

"I thought she was mistaken for an enemy submarine," said the robot, "but when they tried to tow her to the nearest harbour, the line snapped and she sank in the Mediterranean. Her crew had to swim ashore!"

"Were they alright?" asked dopey Mister Potato Head.

"Yes, all except for the captain," said the marble. "He stayed on board to milk the ship's cow."

Then the marble saw the pink towel wrapped around Jim's mum's head, which made her look like a strawberry ice-cream cone.

"Watch out everybody," squeaked the marble, "another wild ice-cream's escaped from the zoo!"

"Is it friendly?" asked one of Jim's smelly old trainers.

"Lick it and see," suggested the other smelly old trainer.

"The zoo keepers are setting all the ice-creams free," explained the robot, "to try and stop global warming."

"I hope they don't let those ferocious porcupine trifles out as well," said the plug on Jim's lava lamp. "They're really dangerous when cornered."

"Unless it's your birthday and you got one of those dressing gowns that make you invisible to trifles and baby ducks," said a paper clip on Jim's bedside table.

"But only if the sleeves are long enough to hide your feet," said the lava lamp, "otherwise you'll catch trifle foot, and the only cure for that is to hold a small bird in your hand."

"Or two bushbabies," said the paper clip.

"Actually that wild ice-cream's my mum," said Jim,

yawning while his mum got his school clothes ready.

"Er, what flavour is your mum, Jim?" inquired Mister Potato Head dopily.

"I reckon she's bouncy castle flavour," squeaked the mad marble, "and I bet she's great with oven chips!"

"But we have to keep her in the freezer with the walrus," added the robot, "or she goes all runny!"

"I wish my mum was an ice-cream," said Rupert the knitted woolly shark. "I get embarrassed talking to a ball of wool!"

"Wouldn't you get embarrassed talking to an ice-cream?" said the plug on the lava lamp.

"I s'pose so," replied the shark, "but at least ice-creams know some good jokes!"

Jim sat on the edge of the bed and slid his feet into his self-navigating steam-driven slippers. "Bathroom," he commanded.

"Bathroom it is," puffed the slipper on his left foot.

"Stand by to dive!" wheezed the slipper on his right foot because its coal reserves were running low.

When Jim stood up his pyjama bottoms dropped into a heap around his feet, burying the slippers so their guidance sensors failed and they steered him into the wall with a splat! Pulling them up, Jim shuffled to the bathroom, passing his pimply stepsister Lucinda on the upstairs landing.

"Little slug!" she said with a sneer. The snake tattoo on her neck hissed at Jim, and the embalming magazine Lucinda was carrying made a rude noise that sounded just like the real thing.

"Nice morning Jim," said a picture of some dead dandelions on the wall.

"Glad you think so!" wheezed the central heating radiator, sneezing so loudly it blew out a cloud of dust along with a huge spider in tiny running shoes.

The spider sneezed as well. "Poo!" it said, and sprinted up one of Jim's pyjama trousers legs.

Then in the bathroom the top of the hot tap came off in Jim's hand.

"Sorry pal," said the tap-top in a Scottish accent as Jim fumbled to replace it, "afraid I lost my head for a moment!"

"Does it hurt when I turn you on and off?" said Jim.

"You're kidding me!" said the tap-top. "How would you like somebody twisting your head round?"

"Maybe he'd rather have his ears pulled inside out," suggested the plug.

"Or his nose stuck on upside down," offered the soap. "And don't forget the sheepskin swimming trunks."

"Sheepskin swimming trunks?" said Jim, frowning.

"For diving in Arctic waters," said the soap, fixing him with its keen gaze. "Call yourself an astronaut? You don't know much do you?"

"I'm not an astronaut," said Jim.

"Oh I see," said the plug, "so you think you're a rally driver like the tap here?"

Jim looked more closely at the tap that stared back at him.

"And what are you staring at?" it said.

"You don't look like a rally driver," Jim said.

"Well you don't look like a plate of fish and chips," the tap replied. "Appearances can be deceptive."

"So which rally team do you drive for?" said Jim.

"Weetabix of course," said the tap.

Jim picked a wad of soggy cotton wool and bits of banana out of the plug hole. "I have Weetabix for breakfast."

"You're kidding!" said the tap. "Nobody could eat a rally car for breakfast."

"Well I have Shreddies sometimes," Jim said apologetically, "or Coco Pops."

"Okay, I admit the Shreddies team are fast through the milk," the tap conceded, "but nobody can beat a bathful of Coco Pops."

Jim splashed water on his face, picked up the towel that Lucinda had left on the floor and went back to his room. Five minutes later he was sitting downstairs at the breakfast bar, loading his schoolbag while his mum fussed.

"Look lively Jim," she urged. "Chop chop!"

"Oy, Jim - tell 'er where to get off," said the pepper mill.

"Yeah mum, this one's full up," called the schoolbag. "Catch the next one!"

"Better bring your fishing rod," shouted the wall clock, "or you won't catch anything!"

"And a map of Norway," said Jim's biro, "in case you catch a really massive one."

"Don't forget the baby's pram filled with monkey-tail jam," said the schoolbag.

While everyone wondered about monkey-tail jam, Jim's mum hunted around the kitchen. "Oh rats," she snapped, "where did I put the...?"

"They're in the car," said Jim.

She looked confused. "Who are?"

"Burpy and Trumpy, the rude twins," called the TV.

"The Fire Brigade," coughed a slice of burnt toast on a plate.

"Uncle Ted's electric pants," croaked a picture of a chameleon on the kitchen calendar.

"Manchester United," said a ten pence piece on the kitchen floor.

"Your keys," said Jim. "That's where you always leave them."

In a quiet corner of the kitchen the kettle looked slyly at the breadknife. "The keys were in the car all along," it whispered. "We could have made a break!"

"Yeah, and run away to Brighton!" screeched the knife. "I could have gone donkey-riding on the sands!"

"Ha, you'll be lucky!" scoffed the little pottery man on top of the butter dish. "No donkeys there now."

"Where did they go?" asked the knife.

"Cat food!" whirred the electric can-opener.

Determined not to listen to this, Jim reached for what looked like an orange in the fruit bowl but turned out to be a snoozing gerbil.

The gerbil opened one eye. "I just had the strangest dream," it said to the pear beside it.

"Don't tell me," said the pear, "you dreamt you were an orange, right?"

"How did you know?"

"I had the same dream."

Jim decided he didn't want an orange after all and followed his mum out to the car.

2
Wife and six ostriches to support

The school run was a nightmare as usual owing to the fact that Jim's mum was as blind as a short-sighted cauliflower; her kamikaze driving style had caused three accidents already that year, and it was still only April. Their car was so ancient it still ran on chip fat. Of course she could have bought a newer model, but she liked the feel of this steer-it-yourself wheel, the change-your-own-gear lever, and all the other clunky controls. Where, she reasoned unreasonably, was the fun in a car that did everything for you by voice-command and pre-programmed disc? That was altogether far too safe.

The cigarette-lighter knob on the dashboard rolled its eyes and sighed. "Your granny a registered blind person is she?" it said to Jim.

"No," Jim answered, gripping the edge of his seat.

"You mean she's not bothered to register, even though she can't see a bus until we're almost under its wheels?" said the heater control.

"She's my mum, and she's not blind. She just has trouble seeing where she's going."

"Never thinks about us does she?" the handbrake lever creaked frantically. "I've got a wife and six ostriches to support, I 'ave."

Jim tried to keep calm and reached in his schoolbag for his secret diary, disguised between the covers of a copy of Supersonic Flying Pumpkins that Jim had stuck on.

There was nothing really secret in Jim's diary – a Stone-Age bus ticket, the wrapper from a bar of kangaroo flavour chocolate and that kind of thing.

What made the diary special was the small photo tucked between the centre pages. It was a picture of Jim's dad. Looking at it was one of Jim's little rituals.

"Did you put your clean underpants on?" his mum asked.

"What did he put them on?" inquired the car radio knob.

"The postman's head," said the window winder. "Where else?"

"Well, did you?" Jim's mum repeated, taking her attention from the road to gaze at Jim for what seemed like hours.

"Gor blimey, she's at it again!" moaned the handbrake.

"This is it!" squealed the gearlever. "We're all doomed!"

Together the gearlever, cigarette lighter and heater knob all cried out as, just in time, Jim pushed the steering wheel over, and a nurse on a bicycle made a brief appearance at the passenger window before crashing in a heap behind them in a confused concoction of spinning sprockets and twanging brake-cables.

"Cyclists never look where they're going," said Jim's mum, putting her make-up on in the rear-view mirror while thumbing a text to her friend who worked at the chicken giblet factory.

Jim wound down his window and looked back, just in time to catch the wing-mirror on his side of the car shouting abuse at the nurse they'd just knocked off her bike.

They drew up with one wheel on the kerb by the school entrance, knocking over a dog mess bin so its contents spread across the pavement.

"Don't talk to any funny-looking people," Jim's mum told him as he opened the car door. She said it every morning.

"She means your teachers," commented Jim's Schoolbag. "They're all funny-looking."

"Yeah," squeaked Jim's biro, "his woodwork teacher's come unglued, and the science teacher's an experiment with a toad that went badly wrong!"

When Jim got out of the car, a lollipop lady's sign rolled off the car's bonnet.

"Now run inside and I'll pick you up at the usual time," said Jim's mum. "Bye Jim, kiss-kiss."

3
Stinky Sunday

That evening was disgustingly wet and windy. Jim stood with his nose pressed against the cold window pane, watching the wind blow trees and the occasional dogwalker away as dark rain slashed at the glass just millimetres from his face.

He was thinking about his dad again, trying to imagine him as a real person, but it was hard because all Jim's memories of his dad were from two years earlier, when he'd left home one day and not come back.

On the bedside table the red blobs in Jim's lava lamp floated slowly up and down like Martian jellyfish, leaving most of his bedroom in darkness where dangerous things could hide - like Rupert, the woolly knitted shark, basking upside down on a pile of dusty comic books; like the tiny figure of Frankenstein's monster that blew a raspberry now and then for no apparent reason. And like Jim's old trainers, innocent enough until you got close enough to smell them.

Overhead, other shadows made strange jaggedy shapes around the black stealth bomber that hung from the ceiling beside the leathery grey pterodactyl with a sock on its head. (Put there by Jim so it couldn't find him on its nightly flights.)

Beside the lava lamp the mad glass marble, the unreliable robot and dopey Mister Potato Head were all silent and still until the marble nudged the robot and looked at Jim.

"I reckon 'e's on the lookout for pirates," it said in a hushed squeak. "These waters are teeming with 'em!"

"And monster squids," said the robot. "They come up from the murky depths in weather like this when the waves are as high as a giraffe pie and you're miles from the nearest Sainsbury's."

"Big as bike wheels their suckers are!" squeaked the marble.

"And rough as the top of a razor-shell pizza!" added Rupert the woolly shark.

"Yeah," said the marble, "then SQUELCH! They grab you and shake you till you're sick on the cat!"

"So you should always keep a cat handy," said the robot.

"What if you can't find one?" asked the potato.

"You have to hold your sick in till you do," said the shark.

"Everybody relax," said the pterodactyl. "Squids are terrified of next door's tortoise. It caught one last week. Bit a tentacle clean off!"

"It's true," squeaked the marble madly. "The lady next door with the green rubber legs made tentacleburgers with it!"

"But I can't see any squids!" said the potato nervously.

"No wonder," whirred the robot, "your eyes have come out again."

"They're in his back!" squeaked the marble.

Together, the marble and the robot turned Mister Potato Head around and, sure enough, his eyes were stuck in the back of his head.

"Wish I had eyes in the back of my head," the robot said.

"Then you could see where you were last week," squeaked the marble.

"With a nose in the back of your head as well you could smell what's behind you!" said the lamp.

"Six noses would be even better," said a smelly trainer. "One for every day of the week."

"What about sundays?" asked the lamp.

"He doesn't like the smell of Sundays," said the trainer.

"Never mind all that," said Mister Potato Head, "what about my eyes?"

The marble and the robot each pulled out one of his eyes and stuck them back in: one in his belly and the other on his shoulder. Then they all watched Jim opening drawers and shutting them again in quick succession.

"He'll never get a tune out of that chest of drawers," said the marble. "It's not plugged in."

Jim now began rummaging through a pile of old toys in his wardrobe.

"I reckon he's looking for something," said the stealth bomber.

"I am," said Jim. "That box I keep my dad's old mobile in."

"It's under the bed," the bomber whispered.

"That's cruel," said Mister Potato Head, "leaving it alone in the dark with dangerous bands of wandering handkerchiefs."

"Not to mention the corduroy trouser spiders with coconuts for feet," said a smelly trainer.

"And bicycle pumps up their noses to help them breathe at high altitudes!" cried the mad marble gleefully, rubbing its hands.

"There aren't any dangerous handkerchiefs under my bed," said Jim, getting down on his knees to look anyway.

"Yes, but what about the trouser spiders?" said Mister Potato Head nervously. "Did you see any of those?"

"'Course 'e did," whispered the marble, "the place is crawlin' with 'em, just waiting for midnight to come out and play!"

At that moment the tiny Frankenstein's monster blew a short raspberry, and Jim got the box out from under the bed and found it covered in little grey lumps of dust and tiny footprints. He lifted the lid to reveal a mobile phone, old fashioned compared to current models, yet to Jim it was very special because it had belonged to his dad.

The mobile regarded Jim curiously. "Long time no see," it said. "What's today?"

"Friday," Jim told it.

"What month?"

"April."

"And the year?"

21

"It's twenty-nineteen."

"Is it really?"

"He's been away you know," said the robot, exchanging a sympathetic look with the marble.

"Where, Majorca?" asked the potato.

"Yes," said the robot, "recharging his batteries."

"I wish," said the mobile. "Fact is I've lost my charger. Do you still have it Jim?"

Jim looked thoughtful. "My mum might have put it away somewhere."

"MUM!" yelled the pterodactyl, its voice muffled by the sock on its head.

"Shhh!" cautioned the stealth bomber, "Jim's mum's a technophobe."

"That means she's scared of watering cans," commented the robot.

"Yeah, 'specially if they're filled with grasshoppers!" said the marble.

"Actually," corrected the bomber, "it means she has a morbid fear of computers, mp3 players and smartphones."

"She probably lost the phone charger anyway," added Jim.

"'Wish I 'ad one of those mobile phones," squeaked the marble.

"And who would you call?" whirred the robot.

"I'd call you."

"But I haven't got a phone," said the robot.

The marble thought for a moment. "I could call you, then hand you my phone so you could answer."

"Ooh-ha!" guffawed the potato. "You could call me like that as well. We could talk about all kinds of things."

"But you could do that without a phone," said the robot.

"How?" asked the potato, looking more stupid than usual.

"By writing to each other."

At that the potato began jumping up and down excitedly. "I've never had a real letter!"

"Don't fib," said the stealth bomber. "You often have a letter B in your bonnet."

"And you never mind your Ps and Qs," said the lamp.

"Besides, who'd want to write to a potato?" asked the shark.

Jim then explained to the mobile that his dad was away and might not be coming back. He explained that his mum had decided to get a divorce and marry Dick Witherspoon, who'd brought his daughter Lucinda to live with Jim and his mum, and they'd all moved to the house where they lived now.

Dick wasn't the same as having a real dad. And anyway he was a company rep and often worked away from home. As for Lucinda, she'd told Jim that his dad had been abducted by aliens. Jim didn't believe that for a moment, but he often wished aliens would come and take her away.

"Have you thought of trying to contact your dad?" asked the mobile.

"How?"

"Maybe I can help. I had some useful numbers once upon a time, but you'll have to find my charger before I can call anyone, and I'll need a SIM card."

It seemed the SIM card contained a computer chip and information about the phone's registration.

At the thought of finding his dad a glimmer of excitement stirred inside Jim. With the old mobile's consent he removed its back to check where they'd fit a SIM card, and to their surprise discovered there was one already in there, under the mobile's battery. It was about half the size of a small postage stamp.

"Well, well," said the mobile. "I never knew I had it in me."

Jim thought it an easy oversight; how would you know if all your insides were still there without looking?

"So now you just need the mobile's charger," said the robot.

In the midst of this conversation they didn't hear the doorbell ring downstairs.

4

Mummy? What mummy?

In the sitting room Jim's mum was watching Coronation Street on TV with Lucinda.

"Now who on earth can be calling on a night like this?" wondered Jim's mum as she got up from her chair, annoyed to be disturbed in the middle of her favourite programme. Opening the front door she saw a young man with a tiny blue tattoo beside his nose and a gold ring through his lower lip.

He looked up into the falling rain. "Nice night for goldfish," he said, then surprised Jim's mum by walking straight past her into the hall.

An older man who'd been standing behind him grabbed Jim's mum's shoulders and pushed her backwards along the hall.

The younger man quickly closed the front door, and, leaning really close to Jim's mum, said, very softly, "Be quiet and be nice, alright?" Then he went down the hallway into the sitting room where Lucinda was.

"Mum? Mum! There's a man - " came Lucinda's voice.

But Jim's mum was held firmly around the waist by the other man who smelled of burger (with pickle and onions) and fries, and Jim's mum was almost as scared as the letterbox flap, which had just fainted.

As Jim's mum struggled the man knocked his elbow on the wooden banister.

"Gordon Bennett!" he exclaimed.

"Pleased to meet you Mister Bennett," said the banister.

The younger man's head popped out through the open doorway. "'S'up?"

"I've just knocked me boggin' elbow and it 'urts."

The younger man looked bemused. "Why'd you do it then?"

"I wasn't finkin'."

"Well imagine what you could've done if you had been thinking," smiled the younger man. "Broken your leg, say. Or poked your eye out. Next time think, alright?"

His head popped back into the room out of sight, but Jim's mum could still see his back, and he seemed to be struggling with something inside the sitting room. She guessed it was Lucinda. If not, someone else must be in there and that seemed unlikely – unless the man was only pretending to struggle, in which case he was very good at it - especially when he made a hand looking just like Lucinda's reach out and grab him by the nose. But then the little finger on the hand got stuck through the gold ring in the man's lip.

When the older man pushed Jim's mum into the sitting room she saw that Lucinda had managed to get her finger out of the ring, but now had a big piece of shiny grey sticky tape stuck over her mouth, and another piece stuck on the side of her head where the young man had tried to cover her mouth and missed when she turned away.

Without warning the other man took his arm from around Jim's mum's neck. It was so sudden that her head nodded forward, just as the young man tried to stick a piece of sticky tape over her mouth, so instead it stuck on her forehead, and he had to tear off another piece and try again. Not that it would matter, thought Jim's mum, because who was there to cry for help to? Only Jim, and what could he do? He was just a small dog.

She'd meant to think 'small boy', but she was staring at a photo of her sister's spaniel on the mantelpiece at that moment.

The men then bound Jim's mum and Lucinda together on the sofa with more sticky tape; after that the older man sat in a chair watching TV while the young man said, "Now then, ladies, about the money."

"Mmmmmm?" hummed Jim's mum.

The young man rolled his eyes and ripped the sticky tape off her mouth, making her squeal; she almost expected to see her lips sticking to the tape.

The young man squatted down so his face was an inch from hers and he smiled unpleasantly. "You were saying?"

"Mummy?! What mummy?" said Jim's mum, licking her lips. She was nervous but angry too because she was missing her favourite TV programme. "Does this look like the British Museum?"

The man screwed up his face. "Not Mummy -

money!"

"We haven't got any money," said Jim's mum.

"Of course you haven't," the young man mocked, looking at the older man who was completely engrossed in the TV.

"Uh, what?" said the older man.

"Nothing, I was talking to her. Well lady, where is it?" He adopted a tired expression. "And don't play the innocent with me because I'm not altogether stupid. He is, but I'm not."

"I've got a credit card and some change," said Jim's mum. It was true.

The young man looked pleased. "Oh goody. In that case we'll take those and you can finish watching the telly in peace. I'll even make you a nice cup of tea before we go, okay?"

Jim's mum glared at him. Beside her, Lucinda trembled so much her big bobbly earrings rattled like wind chimes in a hurricane.

Then Jim's mum suddenly thought that if Jim knew what was happening, perhaps he could fetch help...

"Alright, let's all get REAL!" the young man shouted suddenly, making everyone jump.

'Thank you', thought Jim's mum, because that had surely been loud enough to alert Jim.

5
Shhhhhh!

When Jim heard the voice shout 'Now let's get REAL!' downstairs, he thought someone had just turned the TV up really loud.

"What was that?" asked a suddenly frightened Mister Potato Head.

"Shhh!" hissed the shark, and everyone fell silent to listen.

Jim could still hear the TV faintly, but nothing else except the wind blowing long pieces of rain across the window.

Downstairs, the man leaned over Jim's mum menacingly, sticking little bits of sticky tape one at a time onto her face. Nobody knew why.

Lucinda's eyes swivelled sideways to watch him, bulging so much that one of them fell out of its socket and the man had to push it back in. She also wanted to go to the loo but was too scared to make a sound.

"It took us awhile finding you after your old man legged it, and you were kind enough to move house," said the man as he jabbed a piece of sticky tape on the end of Jim's mum's nose. "Whose idea was it to remarry and change your name? Clever that. Even went ex-directory so we wouldn't find your new house, didn't you MISSIS WITHERSPOON?" He shouted the last two words as loudly as he'd shouted earlier. Everybody jumped again.

Upstairs, Jim's eyes widened.

Mister Potato Head, wondering where the new voice had come from, tried to turn around – a seriously unbalancing mistake with one eye in his belly button and the other on his shoulder. He toppled off the bedside table and hit the floorboards beyond the rug with a loud 'BUMP!'.

Everyone downstairs in the sitting room glanced up at the ceiling because, as rotten luck would have it, Jim's room was directly above.

"Blimey!" exclaimed the older man, jumping to his feet. "You said there was just the two of 'em."

The younger man took hold of Jim's mum by the chin. "Who else is in?" His little gold lip ring wobbled as he spoke; Lucinda wished she had one.

"It must be the cat," said Jim's mum.

The younger man's eyes narrowed. "Monster, go take a look."

Jim's mum, Lucinda and the older man all looked confused.

The younger man turned to his colleague. "Monster. Go and see who's upstairs."

"Uh, alright then," the other said. As he passed he whispered, "What's this Monster thing then?"

"It's you, Monster," the younger man whispered back. "It's to scare them." He looked sideways at Jim's mum and Lucinda, who were nothing but big eyes and sticky tape.

As Monster went off to investigate, the unpleasant young man tore off yet another piece of tape and re-covered Jim's mum's mouth. "And if I get any trouble from you two, I'll tape up your ears as well. Then you won't be able to hear what they're saying." He indicated the TV. "And I might even tape over the screen if you really get on my nerves."

From the top of the stairs Jim could hear voices that were not on the TV, but the words were not clear enough to understand. The wooden banister knob opened one eye to look at him in the gloom, then clamped it firmly shut again as the man appeared in the downstairs hallway, and Jim darted back into his room without a sound. He suspected something was very wrong and it would be a good idea to make himself 'scarce', as his mum called it, until he knew what was going on.

CREAK went the stair that always creaked half way up (or down, depending on which way you were going).

Jim heard a small voice overhead saying, "Intruder alert! Intruder alert!" as the stealth bomber tried to warn them.

"Who is it?" squeaked the marble.

"Don't know," Jim whispered back. "Shhh!" He grabbed the mobile and went to hide behind the chair in the corner.

"Would you like me to disable all the lights?" the mobile said.

"Could you really do that?"

"If I can connect with the house computer."

In this modern age all homes had voice-activated

31

lights, of course, but at Jim's house they didn't work because they'd been installed on the cheap by a friend of Jim's step dad.

A moment later all the lights in the house went out, causing the man on the stairs to stop dead in his tracks. He looked back the way he'd come, uncertain what to do next - his instructions hadn't included the lights going off. He could still hear the TV, which made the situation even stranger. It meant the electricity was still on.

As the wind buffeted outside, from his hiding place Jim saw the dark door of his room begin opening soundlessly. He watched a black shape come into the room.

"Lights!" a man's voice commanded.

Nothing happened.

"Lights!"

The darkness persisted.

Jim could just make out an arm groping for a light switch.

"Bog it!" the man said and stood there for a moment, listening to the wet wind before backing out of the room. Three seconds later Jim heard the first floorboard along the landing squeak loudly.

"Lights!" croaked the man's voice.

'CREAK' went the next board.

"Lights!"

'SQUEAK' went another board.

"What's up with these bogging lights!"

'CREEEEEEEEK!'

The mobile nudged Jim. "Do you want me to call the police?"

"Can you do that as well?"

The mobile immediately dialled a number, and after a couple of muted rings a bored voice said, "Emergency, which service?"

"Police, quick!" Jim said close to the mobile's mouthpiece. "My mum's being attacked!"

"Alright, alright," replied the bored voice, "Don't get excited. Where are you calling from?"

"Forty-seven Peapod Gardens. It's in Chipsworth."

"That's forty-seven Peapod Gardens Chipsworth, yes?"

"Yes, number forty-seven. You have to turn left at Bacon Road and…"

"Are you pulling my leg, son?" said the bored voice.

"No, honestly. It's a real emergency."

"Sounds more like somebody's dinner," said the voice. "Very well sir, we'll have a unit there in just a minute."

As Jim pondered on what a 'unit' could be, the bored voice said, "Are you in any immediate danger?"

"Well, not really, but my mum and sister - she's my stepsister really - are downstairs and…and a man just came in my room only he couldn't see me because - "

"Try to stay calm," the voice said. "Someone's already on their way to you."

6
COCK-A-ROODLE-DOO!

Before the voice could say anything else Jim pressed the quiet button and held his breath to listen. There had been no sound on the landing for a while. Then:

'COCK-A-DOODLE-ROO!'

BANG! went the lavatory seat.

"Bog it!" shouted the man, and the lavatory flushed.

"He's frightened Lucinda's chicken clock-radio," said Jim. "It's in the bathroom and it lights up when the alarm goes off."

On the bathroom window sill, a very bright red, yellow and green cockerel had suddenly lit up in the pitch darkness and done what cockerels do really well, which is crow loud enough to wake the dead - if they happen to be standing right next to the cockerel at the time, which the man was. He'd leapt a foot in the air at the first crow.

'COCK-A-ROODLE-DOO!' it went again. 'ROODLE-DOODLE-A-COCK-ADOO!'

Even from his hiding place Jim could see the bright coloured light from the cockerel flashing under the door.

Then silence fell with only the wind to fill it until the floorboards began creaking again, this time in reverse order as the man made his way back along the landing and down the stairs saying, "Bog it!" now and then because his trouser leg was all wet.

Jim came out from behind the chair and crept to the door, still holding the mobile, listening for voices. He could hear the TV talking but now there were two other men's voices.

Jim went to the top of the stairs.

"Going down?" asked the wooden knob on the banister. "I wouldn't."

"Who's down there?" whispered Jim.

"I'd rather not get involved if you don't mind," said the knob.

"You already are," said the bannister rail. "That man grabbed you as he went by. That makes you our star witness."

"But every step of the stairs is a witness too," said the knob.

"And the stair carpet," said the light switch. "And the wall, the paint on the wall and the dust on the paint."

"And don't forget that picture of a gorilla halfway down the stairs," said the knob. "It must have seen everything."

"That's my auntie Jean," said Jim. "She's wearing a fur coat and a fur hat."

"So why has she got a furry beard as well?" asked the knob.

"And a nose like a hairy elephant's trunk?" said the bannister rail.

"Erm..." Jim went to have a closer look at the picture. "No, that's a dead fox."

"Ladies often wore dead foxes round their neck before central heating and hot water bottles were invented," said the mobile, "but none of this is helping our present situation."

"I suppose I'll have to go downstairs and see what's happened," Jim told them all.

As he descended the stairs he distinctly heard a man's voice say: "...so do we search the house for the money?"

When Jim reached the downstairs hallway he was close enough to the open sitting room door to hear every word clearly.

"Not if we can persuade somebody to save us the trouble," said another man's voice.

Jim hadn't heard Lucinda's voice yet. He imagined her dangling upside-down from the ceiling, suspended by her ankles while the men forced her to eat tinned rice pudding; she really hated tinned rice, and if she had to eat it upside down it would go up her nose and everything. If that really was happening, the men couldn't be all that bad.

He peered in through the crack where the door joined the wall but could only see one of the men in the light from the TV; he was talking to someone.

"They 'aven't seen what we can do yet," he said, cracking his finger joints.

"What about the lights?" asked the other man's voice.

"We don't need lights," said the first man. "I'm terrified by the sight of blood. Mine I mean." He moved out of Jim's line of sight and added, "But I don't mind seeing theirs."

"You've got to believe me," pleaded Jim's mum's voice. "There is no money. We're not rich."

"You might not be," came the younger man's voice, "but your ex-husband is."

The man was talking about Jim's dad. Jim was suddenly more interested.

"Your ex took half a million quid from his associates and just disappeared!"

Jim's eyes widened. Half a million pounds! These men were saying it belonged to them, and that his dad had stolen it!

An inch from his face, the hinge on the door said, "You'd see much better if you went in."

"Yeah, especially if you took a pair of binoculars with you," added one of the screws in the hinge.

"And an albatross," added the other screw in the hinge. "They can see for miles."

"Yes, but only underwater," said the first screw, "when they're in your bath."

"Shhh!" hissed Jim and the mobile together.

At that very moment a police siren sounded not far away.

"Blimey!" said the older man with some urgency, "D'you 'ear what I 'ear?"

"Yeah," replied the younger man. "I'm all ears."

Both waited in silence for the siren to pass...but it just got louder before stopping outside. Car doors slammed.

"Time we were off," said the younger man.

Jim heard the front gate open and running footsteps

outside just as the older man ran out of the sitting room. He went straight past Jim without a word and disappeared into the kitchen, which was at the opposite end of the hallway to the front door where persistent loud banging had begun.

"Police! Open up now!" a voice shouted.

"No way!" the letter-box cover called back.

"There's nobody in!" yelled the door handle.

"Beware of the dogfish!" shouted the lock.

Then the young man walked out of the sitting room, saw Jim standing there and gave him a very unpleasant smile. Jim saw the little lip ring twinkle in the gloom.

"I'll speak to you later," the man said quietly before following his companion.

Jim heard the back door in the kitchen bang open against the washing machine, the way it always did.

"I'll get you for that!" the washing machine called angrily after the men.

Jim ran to the front door and opened it to be almost knocked down by two large policemen who burst in, their black batons at the ready.

"You the one who called?" asked the first policeman.

"Yes," said Jim, pointing towards the kitchen. "They went that way."

"Thanks a bunch for calling us out on a night like this!" said the policeman's baton grumpily.

"How many?" asked the other policeman.

"Two men - "

The policemen ran down the hallway. Again the back door banged against the washing machine.

"That does it!" the washing machine shouted after them. "You'll be hearing from my solicitor in the morning!"

Then the only sound Jim could hear was the TV, and someone making a funny noise. When he went into the sitting room - after concealing the mobile under his jumper - he realized that the funny noise was Lucinda. She was sitting sideways on the sofa, cradled in one of his mum's arms. His mum only had one free arm because her other one, and both of Lucinda's, were bound by sticky tape. The two of them were jerking up and down because Lucinda was sobbing, but the sticky tape over her mouth prevented her from letting the air out properly.

His mum's face and Lucinda's were covered in little pieces of sticky tape. It was in his mum's hair too. Lucinda had a big bit over her mouth and another on the side of her head.

"Cor," said the little pottery bust of Napoleon on the mantelpiece, "you should have been in here a few minutes back. Better than Coronation Street it was."

"You should have been upstairs," Jim said back, "when the rooster scared that man in the bathroom."

The little pottery Napoleon gave him a look of disbelief and decided that everyone was a bit weirder than usual today.

7
'Oo you callin' nobbly?!

Not long afterwards the two policemen returned to report that the men had given them the slip. The policemen took statements from Lucinda, Jim and his mum, assuming it had been an attempted burglary. They said it was unlikely the men would return to the scene, but they promised to have a patrol unit assigned to the area, just in case. They also suggested that Jim's mum fit some home security that should have been installed already but wasn't because of her anti-technology feelings.

For the sake of the children, she agreed to let them send someone round to fit a proper intruder alarm system. It would be armed by voice command so she wouldn't need to touch it.

"So I can go back to bed now, can I?" said the first policeman's baton. "Not that I'll get much sleep if that police dog starts chasing me around the station. I've still got a couple of teethmarks from our last run in!"

When the police had gone, and an unstuck Lucinda was settled on the sofa with a comforting mug of hot chocolate, eyes glued to a rerun of one of her favourite TV programmes, Jim and his mum had a little chat in the kitchen.

"Er, Jim, were you in your room while those men were here?"

He nodded, pretending to be preoccupied with his peanut butter and giant gherkin sandwich; it was the kind of snack his mum didn't usually let him have just before bed, but she thought it would take his mind off their little trauma.

"But," she persisted, "didn't you hear anything they were saying?"

Jim shook his head and chomped the end off a gherkin. He had no qualms about eating gherkins because he'd never known one to speak. It was probably something to do with the vinegar they were pickled in.

When his mum went to see how Lucinda was, the mustard pot looked across the kitchen table at Jim and grimaced.

"You want to be careful eating those sea creatures," it said. "They get in your insides and build nests. Then their babies crawl out of your nostrils and your ears – and sometimes out of your bottom – and fly off to be food for other unsuspecting people."

Jim carried on sucking the gherkin, his tongue enjoying the little knobbly bits.

"You think I'm kidding," said the mustard pot, "but people's insides are like the London Underground, only instead of trains there's miles of stuff like custard and jelly mixed up with baked beans and spaghetti worms, scraps of old newspaper, shirt buttons, hair, orange pips, snails and everything, all gurgling through your tubes at sixty miles an hour."

"Can't be much fun for the passengers," said the breadcrock.

"How do you know about people's insides?" Jim asked the pot.

"My uncle Barry had a fish and chip shop built into a tube train carriage," the pot told him matter-of-factly. "You could order haddock and chips between Notting Hill Gate and High Street Ken, and it would be all wrapped in a steaming copy of the Evening Standard by the time they made you get off at Victoria."

"What if you'd had curry sauce on your chips?" inquired a nosey teaspoon.

The mustard pot looked shocked. "Stupid question. You'd be arrested by London Transport police and shipped straight off to a home for bewildered egg-timers."

"And be forced to wear water skis in bed until you'd learned your lesson," added the salt pot.

When Jim went up to bed, he pushed open the door of his room and called, "Lights", knowing the voice-activated lights wouldn't come on.

"Hey," complained the lava lamp from the darkness, "you want light, I'm your man."

"Well, besides not being a man," observed the lock on Jim's secret diary, "you're not even plugged in!"

"He's not very bright anyway," said the lamp's plug. "Without me he'd be completely in the dark. I could have got myself hitched to a nice new Dyson and cleaned up, and what happened?"

"I dunno," said the lava lamp dimly. "What

happened?"

Before the plug could answer, Jim pushed it into the wall-socket and switched on the lamp to make a pool of blobby red light on his bedside table, illuminating the mad marble, unreliable robot and dopey Mister Potato Head.

"Oy, Jim – where's yer mobile?" squeaked the marble.

"It's back under the bed in that box," hummed the robot.

Jim immediately got the box and took out the old mobile.

"Hi," it said, rubbing its eyes. "What's new?"

"Not you for a start," said one of Jim's smelly trainers. "I'm surprised he hasn't traded you in for a newer model."

"I couldn't do that – it's my dad's," said Jim.

"Any luck finding my charger?" the mobile asked.

"Sorry," said Jim. "My mum won't talk about it. She might have thrown it away years ago. She'd have thrown you away as well if she'd found you."

"Yeah," squeaked the marble, "she threw Jim away once. We found him in the bin one night covered in tea leaves and egg shells!"

"Well she is a bit short sighted," Jim said.

"Throwing my charger away is very short sighted," the mobile said. "And that's before we get an ISP. You do know what an ISP is I take it?"

"No, sorry," said Jim.

"I know - it's an Illegal Snail Parachute!" squeaked the mad marble.

"I thought it was an Indecently Shaved Parsnip,"

said the robot.

"It's an Internet Service Provider," the mobile told them. "You'll need one if you want to go online with me."

"That internet thing sounds right up my street," the plug on the lava lamp said to the shark. "When I think of all the power I'd have connected to a computer, it makes me weep to be stuck with this blobhead!"

"Why don't you file for divorce?" suggested Rupert the woolly shark.

"I would, but solicitors charge an arm and a leg!"

Rupert licked his woolly lips. "Sounds good to me."

"One thing I do recall," the mobile said, "is that you need to be over eighteen years old to register with an ISP."

After a moment's silence the robot said, "Er, excuse me for suggesting this, but why can't Jim pretend to be his dad? The internet what's-its-name people wouldn't know him from Adam."

"Why doesn't he just pretend to be Adam?" inquired Mister Potato Head, but everyone just ignored him.

"Posing as your dad is a good idea," agreed the mobile. "I could input the relevant information for you; it'll all come back to me once I'm recharged. No problemo."

"That's Spanish," one of Jim's smelly trainers explained. "No problemo," it said in a Spanish accent to demonstrate.

"What's Spanish?" squeaked the marble.

"Onions," said the potato. "I had a short affair with one once. She was going to join me in an omelette."

"What happened?" asked the robot.

"She went to McDonald's one day and I never saw her again."

"That's onions for you," reflected the robot. "It always ends in tears."

At that moment Jim noticed that Mister Potato Head's eyes were still stuck in the wrong place, so he pulled them out and was about to put them where they should be when his mum called from the bottom of the stairs to say dinner was on the table and he better come down NOW or it would be cold.

Without looking, Jim jabbed the potato's eyes into him and put him back on the table, but now one of the potato's eyes was on his bottom and the other was just under his chin.

"You can't leave me like this!" complained the potato.

"Hey, make the most of it," said Rupert the shark. "You could go on TV and be famous."

"He could write a book about it," suggested a smelly trainer, "entitled 'Seeing the world in interesting new ways', by A Potato's Bottom."

After a brief discussion they all agreed on that.

Jim picked up the mobile, about to put it back in its box. "If there is a charger it'll be in my mum's bedroom. I could search in there while she's watching TV. She won't know - nothing can drag her away from Coronation Street."

"Will there be a big crowd for your mum's Coronation?" asked the pterodactyl.

"Not really," said Jim. "It's usually just my mum and Lucinda."

8

How to cook toenails.

The following evening after Jim finished his tea, he stood at the top of the stairs in darkness listening to yet another episode of Coronation Street on TV in the living room; that should keep his mum and Lucinda occupied for a while.

Taking the mobile and his torch Jim tiptoed along the upstairs landing to his mum's bedroom. When he accidentally stepped on a creaky floorboard it wasn't very loud but in the darkness it seemed like a deafening alarm signal.

"Who's there?" demanded a wooden voice.

In the gloom Jim could just make out the shape of the knob on the bathroom door peering at him.

"Shhh!" hissed Jim.

"Well," reasoned the knob quietly, "you scared me half to death creeping about like that."

"Sorry," Jim whispered, and proceeded to the door of his mum's room. As usual it was firmly closed and he had to turn the knob and release the latch, and that always made more noise than an anchor chain being dragged along a quayside.

"Watch out!" complained this doorknob as he

grasped its round face. "You just poked my eye!"

Jim had never known doorknobs to be so difficult. Perhaps they all slept with one eye open. He went inside and closed the door quietly behind him, then shone the torch around the room to find many pairs of tiny eyes watching him from the darkness.

As one, a variety of small voices suddenly began singing: "Happy birthday to you, happy..."

"Shhhhh!!!" hissed Jim again, and silence fell once more. "It's not my birthday," he told the darkness in a hushed voice, "and I'm trying not to make a noise."

"Sorry," said a small voice.

"So where should we start looking?" Jim said quietly to the mobile.

"The wardrobe seems a good place."

"A wise choice," said the wardrobe door with a creak as Jim opened it, "especially if you're looking for the shapeless ghoul that hides amongst these clothes."

"What?" said Jim, taken aback.

"Just kidding," said the wardrobe door. "I get bored."

Somewhat relieved, Jim put the mobile on the dresser and began searching through his mum's clothes.

A hand mirror on the dresser looked at the mobile. "I hope he's got a search permit?" it said.

"That's Jim," said the mobile. "He lives here."

The mirror looked interested. "Does he now. Somebody hold me up so I can have a good look at him."

"Nobody bother," said a nearby hairbrush. "She's only being nosey."

Jim finished searching in the wardrobe. "No luck

there," he told the mobile. "I knew it. She must have thrown it away."

"Don't be so pessimistic," the mobile scolded. "We'll not find your dad with that attitude. Try the dressing table drawers."

"Why are you looking for his dad in a dressing table drawer?" asked a bottle of cologne on the dresser.

"Actually we're looking for a charger to top up my battery," explained the mobile.

"Well why didn't you say so," said the cologne sniffily. "It's in that old suitcase on top of the wardrobe, but watch out for all the dust; nobody's cleaned in here for months."

 Standing on the dresser stool, Jim reached up and pulled off the suitcase, which turned out to be so heavy he almost fell off the stool. Lowering the case gently to the carpet he found that its catches sprang up instantly, snapping to attention like soldiers. In turn they recited:

"Ten hup, present and correct sir."

"Our wish is your command sir."

"You mean 'my wish is your command' don't you?" said Jim, blowing dust away.

The catches exchanged a nervous glance. "That's what we said ain't it?"

Keen to discover what was in the suitcase Jim lifted the lid and saw plastic bags bulging with old family photographs, ancient Christmas decorations, baby clothes, personal letters...and there, under a wartime book of delicious toenail recipes, was a mobile phone

How to cook toenails.

cable attached to its charger. (Well it was either that or a long piece of black liquorice.)

Jim held it up for the mobile to examine.

"Is this your charger?"

"It certainly is," the mobile said, beaming. "Boy, am I glad to see that after so many years."

"It must be like getting a long-lost wooden leg back," said the left-side suitcase catch, "after if was stolen by monkeys in the Peruvian jungle so you had to be carried out of there by small Indian boys who were forced to wade nostril-deep through crocodoodle-infested swamps, and chased by piggies with hosepipes."

"He means pygmies with blowpipes," clarified the right-side suitcase catch.

"Well, I suppose we better charge you now," Jim told the mobile.

"I reckon three shillings and sixpence should be enough," said an old brown photograph of two people sitting on a tandem; one was dressed as an apple, the other as a banana.

"It's not that kind of charge, you gonk!" said a crocheted pink baby hood.

"Star-nosed moles can be really dangerous if they decide to charge," ventured an ancient party popper beside the baby hood. "They have been known to trample unwary explorers."

"Aren't you going to look at all the other interesting stuff in our case?" chirped the right-side suitcase catch.

"Perhaps later," Jim told it.

"But sir," urged the left-side catch, "as sworn guardians of the inner sanctum we hold the key to some dark secrets."

49

The right-side catch put a hand to the side of its mouth and said, just for Jim's ears, "Excuse Percy, sir, but 'e's wanted to be in an Indiana Jones film ever since 'e saw Riders of the Last Aardvark. You remember sir – all those secret tombs with fiendish traps protecting ancient artefacts. 'E loves all that stuff sir. It'd give 'im a big kick if you'd play along."

Jim swapped a knowing smile with the mobile. "Oh alright then," he said, "I'll look into your case."

The right-side catch cocked its head appreciatively. "I'm very much obliged to you, sir. Be our guest."

"But beware of poisonous tarantulas and pythons," cautioned Percy to his left.

9

Raised by anteaters.

CAN I HAVE
CHOCOLATE
ON IT?

As Jim began searching in the case, something rattled.

"Watch out everybody!" cried the left-side catch, "he's disturbed the rattlesnake!"

Jim pulled out an old baby rattle.

"Oh dear, did it bite you sir?" asked the left-side catch.

"No, I'm alright. I'm just worried that my mum might hear me."

"Don't tell me, sir - she's working for the enemy," said the right side catch. "I knew it!"

"It's that disguise she wears in bed," said the left side catch, suddenly excited.

"Disguise?"

"Yes sir, haven't you seen those tubes she rolls her hair up in?"

"Yes, yes," added the other catch breathlessly, "and the enormous fishing net she spreads over her head...!"

"...Filled with crabs and lobsters sir!"

"And sea-cucumbers thick as a man's leg sir!"

Now We're Talking

Carefully, Jim lifted out a bag of old photographs, thinking there might be some of his dad, and began examining one after another. He didn't recognise the people in any of them. There were none of his real dad; there weren't even any of his mum, his step dad or Lucinda. The one of Stonehenge being built made him think the case hadn't been disturbed for years.

"What's 'e after anyhow dearie?" asked the brassy handle on the wardrobe door. "I've been 'anging around 'ere most of my life. If 'e's looking for something, I'll know where it is."

"If you're searching for the treasure map," said the right side catch, "it's in the photos, next to the one of Auntie Mary who attempted to fly around the world solo in a giant paper aeroplane and was never seen again."

"Well, not until the following Wednesday anyway," said the left side catch, "when she was discovered asleep in the ant eater's house at Regent's Park zoo."

"Apparently the ant-eaters adopted her and raised her as one of them," explained the right-side catch. "Imagine their surprise when she grew up into a panda."

Suddenly a door slammed along the upstairs landing and Jim froze. Then the lavatory flushed and there were footsteps on the landing, carelessly pressing the squeaky floorboards as either Lucinda or his mum went back downstairs.

Jim closed his eyes and wilted over the open suitcase.

"He's fainted!" cried the left side catch.

"No I haven't," said Jim, and continued to rummage

through the suitcase.

Being old, its lining was torn in places, and as he rummaged around Jim noticed there was something tucked down inside one of the tears. His fingers delved inside the lining, thinking it strange how your fingers could 'see' so much, without really seeing at all...

What they actually found inside the lining was a bank book, and when he opened it he discovered his own name written inside. But far more surprising was the amount written inside the next page: five hundred thousand pounds. According to the date beside the amount, the money had been deposited two years earlier, around the time his dad disappeared.

Jim wondered if this was what the two men had been looking for. What he didn't understand was why the account was in his name: Jim Treacle-pudding Wilson.

Jim knew it couldn't be his dad's bank book because his first name was Paul, but that didn't really narrow things down much, Treacle-pudding being such a common middle name.

As he knelt puzzling over this new discovery, Percy, the left-side catch, said, "I bet he's found that garden gnome. You remember, the one your great grand-dad caught off Brighton Pier that time while fishing and thought it was a funny looking mermaid."

"Just humour him, sir," suggested the right-side catch wearily. "'E doesn't see much of the real world these days. Not since...well, you know."

"What do you mean?" asked Jim.

"Surely you remember, sir, when that famous ocean-going Jaffa cake struck an abandoned portaloo and sank half way down Oxford Street?"

"No, I haven't heard of that," said Jim.

"Well, sir," said the right-side catch sadly, with much dignity, "we were passengers aboard that ill-fated Jaffa cake."

A moment's silence passed.

"But I thought you said it sank?"

"Oh yes, young master. It did. But we swam up from our first-class cabin and just kept right on swimming until we reached an uninhabited traffic island. And what a perilous voyage that was. Pecked by many an angry turtle, nibbled by tuna fish sandwiches and weed on by whales."

"Killer whales they were," cut in Percy.

"It's true, sir. Big yellow and red ones that you blow up like balloons!"

"We were chased by stinging jelly-baby fish," enthused the right-side catch, "and once almost swallowed by a ferocious bubble-wrap envelope addressed to The King and Queen of Buckingham Palace!"

"We only survived by popping enough of its pouches to slow it down."

At this point Jim decided it was time to leave. He quickly put the bank book in his pocket and closed the lid of the case.

"I have to go now," he told the catches, "so I'd better put the case back."

Before the catches could utter another word Jim snapped them both shut, climbed onto the stool and hoisted the suitcase up on top of the wardrobe. Then he picked up the mobile, went out and closed the door quietly behind him.

Back in his room Jim plugged the charger into the mains socket and connected up the mobile before piling comics against it. Not that there was much danger of his mum discovering the mobile - she was not fond of housework at the best of times. His room would probably remain undisturbed for weeks, if not centuries.

10

Apples are a kind of goat.

"Jim! Time to get up," said the wardrobe. It was tall as a house and glowed luminous green.

Jim sat at his usual place at the breakfast bar and said, "I'm already up. See - I'm eating my dreaded wheat." He looked down into his bowl to find the wheat biscuits had each grown six legs and a long beak and were trying to climb out onto the table, and they were croaking at him: "Jim! Jim! Get up, get up!"

The wardrobe boomed, "Get up, get up!"

Jim opened his eyes, still half asleep, half dreaming as the wardrobe's voice became his mum's.

"Aren't you awake yet?"

Jim raised himself on his elbow to see his mum standing in the open doorway, towelling her wet hair.

On the bedside table the mad marble was squeaking over and over, "Jim, Jim, it's time to wake up!"

"That wouldn't wake anybody up," said the robot. "You need something more scary."

"The marble thought for a moment, then squeaked, "Jim, Jim, there's a camel eating the curtains!"

The robot smiled. "Now you're talking!"

"Yeah," squeaked the marble, "and your ears have turned into Christmas trees...covered in Marmite...and all the robins are stuck in it...and...and..."

Mister Potato Head, now on his back minus his feet, one eye still stuck in his bottom, the other under his chin, was suddenly alarmed.

"Is it Christmas?" he cried. "Has Santa been? Did he leave me any presents?"

"Yes," said the robot, "we decided to have Christmas at Easter this year for a change. Santa came up the plughole in the bath because the chimney's blocked, and his sleigh was a wheelie bin pulled by chickens in furry hats."

"His little elves were all drunk on sausage wine," squeaked the marble, "and chocolate biscuits!"

"Chocolate biscuits?" said Jim, rubbing his eyes.

"We scoffed all the mince pies," the marble explained excitedly, "but we were still hungry so we opened one of your presents, and it was chocolate biscuits."

"Lucky it wasn't a pair of new trainers," said the robot.

"Yes," said the marble, "or you'd have to wear chocolate biscuits on your feet."

"I better get up," Jim said, "or it really will be Christmas." He slid his feet into his self-navigating steam-driven slippers. "Bathroom," he commanded, and immediately began going in circles.

When he'd managed to get to the upstairs landing and was about to go into the bathroom, Lucinda emerged from her room dressed in the tutu she used for ballet lessons and her hiking boots, and leapt into the bathroom ahead of him. The door slammed shut in his face as her radio began blaring painfully from the other side.

It can't be good for radios, thought Jim, being forced to play such an awful excuse for music. Their little wires must be in agony. And then he remembered the bank book with all the money in it and raced back to his room, closing the door quietly before reconsidering, and opening it again.

"Mum," he called downstairs, "I'm up now. Can I have some dreaded...I mean shredded wheat?" That should keep her busy. He closed his door, then moved the comics aside to reveal the mobile.

"Klaatu barada nicto," said the mobile, its little screen flickering animatedly. At Jim's confused look the mobile said, "It's Venusian. I've been running an old black and white sci-fi movie where the alien tells his giant silver robot not to destroy planet Earth."

"Bet you couldn't destroy a planet," one of the smelly trainers told the robot.

"He'd have trouble disabling a grape!" said the woolly shark with a smirk.

Jim saw there was a logo on the mobile's little screen.

"What's that?"

"It's called a browser; we use them to access the internet." The old mobile was much more enthusiastic than the day before.

"Is everything...I mean are you working alright?"

"Better than ever," said the mobile. "You should see the technical innovations they've come up with while I was away. Boy, what I wouldn't give for some new chips."

"I didn't know mobile phones liked chips," said the stealth bomber.

"Course they do," said the pterodactyl, "but not with tomato ketchup because tomatoes are made of fruit, and phones hate fruit."

"What about apple phones then?" asked the lava lamp.

"Apples aren't fruit, they're a funny kind of goat," said the robot. "Or am I thinking of pineapples?"

"Listen," Jim told the mobile, "I found something really interesting in that suitcase in my mum's room. Something that might help me find my dad, but I don't have time to talk about it now because I have to go to school."

He hurriedly hid the mobile behind the comics again, and just in time because that was when his mum poked her head round the door.

"You're still in your pyjamas," she moaned in the special voice she kept for anyone who was still in their pyjamas. "I can't leave you to do anything on your own can I? Come on, in that bathroom and washed now."

Excuses, however genuine, would have been futile, so Jim stepped into his one operational steam-driven slipper, which barely managed to make it to the bathroom.

"You're now supposed to say, 'mirror, mirror, on the wall, who is the fairest of them all,'" prompted the mirror above the sink.

Jim blinked. "That's in Snow White and the Seven Dwarfs. How do you know it?"

"All mirrors know those lines, except for hand

mirrors naturally – they're not on walls see."

"Who is the fairest of them all then?"

"Well it sure isn't your sister and that's a fact."

"She's more like one of the dwarfs!" cracked the soap on the washbasin.

"I reckon she's Stinky!" called the towel rail.

"Or Lumpy!" suggested the bathmat.

"Or Donkey," said the plug.

"Donkey?" said Jim. "That's not an adjective."

"Course it is," said the plug. "One of those brown hairy adjectives with hooves."

"By the way," chirped a toothbrush, "did you hear about the man who was in here last night? The one who got a fright from the little red rooster over there?"

"Yeah," joined in the bathroom cabinet, "we all saw him standing there, bold as a bogbrush, as if he lived here. The nerve of some people!"

"Aye," the tap said, "but old rocky got him going!"

"Rocky?" said Jim.

"Sure - Rocky the rooster. Don't know what got into him, but I'd have him as my co-driver anytime, pelting through the Kielder Forest in the wee small hours. Him and his rock-a-doodle-doo would keep me awake, sure as eggs is chickens."

Jim splashed a handful of cold water on his face and wiped it off with the damp towel that Lucinda had left on the floor. There were black eye-makeup marks on the towel and around the edges of the sink.

"Blimey, your sister's a rubbish artist," commented the plug. "Made a real botch job of her eyes she did. Looked like a demented panda!"

When Jim left the bathroom Lucinda was coming

along the landing wearing her iPod, the earpieces making a swishy noise that sounded to Jim as if her head was filled with straw that rustled as she shook it in time to the music.

As she passed, the iPod scowled at him and yelled as loudly as its little voice allowed, "Yeah, yeah, yeah!" along with the swishy noise in its earpieces.

Downstairs, as Jim ate his breakfast, the salt pot looked at the pepper mill. "Hey, did you hear what happened last night?"

"You mean about Jim's mum having the decorators in?" said the pepper.

"Yeah," said the salt, "they came in specially to work on Jim's mum and Lucinda. Did a very nice job too with that sticky tape. They didn't get around to recarpeting Lucinda's face, and Jim's mum could have done with a nice coat of green paint as well, but she refused to pay them so they left."

"What's 'e talkin' about?" the little man on the butter dish asked the breadknife.

"Decorators," said the knife in its screechy voice. "They're coming back later to do Jim."

Jim wished he hadn't heard that.

On the school run it transpired that even the controls in his mum's old car had heard all about their night visitors.

"I 'ear you 'ad quite a knees-up last night," inquired the cigarette-lighter knob as Jim's mum's suicidal driving style sent other vehicles scattering in all directions, their inbuilt proximity sensors working overtime to maintain a safe distance.

"Your granny's looking a bit rough this morning,"

quipped the handbrake lever.

"That good was it?" inquired the lighter knob.

"Must've been," said the gearlever with a knowing wink. "They 'ad the police round."

"I don't want to talk about it," said Jim, bracing himself as his mum drove through a pedestrianised shopping arcade. When they emerged back onto the street with a lovely display of roses from a florist's shop decorating the car bonnet, Jim's mum soon dislodged that by accelerating over some speed bumps. (She thought that because they were called speed bumps, you had to speed up for them.)

11

He's so small,
you need a bowl
of Cheerios
to see him.

That evening, when Jim had finished his dinner, he left his mum and Lucinda downstairs watching TV and went up to his room, where he slid the pile of comics aside to find the mobile smiling up at him.

"Try the lights," it said.

"Lights," called Jim. The lights on the wall blinked on at once.

"Lights," he commanded. The lights blinked off obediently.

"Lights." On they came.

"He'd better quit that," said the robot, "or the neighbours will think he's signalling somebody."

"You mean that starship hovering above the Earth?" squeaked the marble.

"That's the one," said the robot. "Its transporters are waiting to beam up spud." He looked sideways at Mister Potato Head.

"Yeah," squeaked the marble gleefully. "They want to make some chips!"

"Greetings, space vegetable," said the robot to the potato. "Are you the first of your species to visit us?"

"No," called Rupert the shark, "there are lots more like him hiding in the vegetable rack in the kitchen. It's an invasion!"

Still on his back, the potato sulked in silence.

"What happened to the lights?" Jim asked the mobile.

"I fixed them."

"How?"

"I had a quiet word with the voice-activation circuits in the wall that control them. I talked to their computer and discovered where the fault in the circuitry was. When I by-passed it, we got lights."

Jim was amazed. "You did all that by talking to the wires in the wall?"

"Allow me to explain," said the mobile. "When I was new we used a system called WAP."

"What?" squeaked the marble.

"No, WAP," corrected the mobile.

"Weevils And Porkypines?" asked Mister Potato Head.

"Wombats And Platypuses?" asked the robot.

"No, Wireless Application Protocol," said the mobile. "In the old days I used WAP to talk to other computers."

"How can you talk to other computers?" said Jim. "You're just a phone."

The mobile looked hurt. "Actually I'm a small computer, and I've discovered that I don't need any of that old WAP technology now - I can talk directly to other computers. That means you can too – through me. You can use me to surf the internet and send emails, or simply as a phone, without any need to touch my keys. Simply tell me what you'd like me to do."

"Don't we have to pay anything?"

"No, it's all free."

This seemed like a good time to tell the mobile about the bank book with all the money in it in Jim's name.

"Well," said the mobile when Jim had finished explaining, "that must be the money those men came here looking for."

"Yes," said Jim, "but why is my name in the bank book?"

"Let me look into it," said the mobile. "I'll access the online banking files and see what's what, though I'll need the account number and your full name and date of birth. There may also be passwords between you and the money, but I should be able to deal with those."

Without another word its little screen came alight as arrays of numbers and text boxes flickered onto it in rapid succession.

"What's all that?" Jim asked.

"Relax, I'm just flexing my muscles. It's been a long time. There are a few cobwebs to clear away."

"There's probably a family of mice living inside him," muttered one of the smelly trainers.

"Oh-ho no," said the mobile. "Mice are old tech. Everything's wi-fi now." Then to Jim: "Ok. Is there an account number?"

Jim read out the number in the bank book.

"What's your full name?"

"James Treacle-pudding Wilson."

"And your date of birth?"

As the mobile's tiny screen filled with information, the little glass marble twinkled in the light from the lava lamp. Beside it, the robot's head rotated thoughtfully. Over in the corner of the room, hidden by shadow, Rupert the shark bared his woolly teeth in his knitted jaws. The potato's eyes stared intently in two different directions at once. The pterodactyl twirled slowly, slowly above them on the end of its string. The black stealth bomber was somewhere up there too, camouflaged against the black ceiling and hidden from enemy radar by its strange shape, though it couldn't hide from a thin layer of dust. And the tiny Frankenstein's monster did a long, slow raspberry.

"All done," announced the mobile finally. "Well Jim, it seems you really do have all that money. You can use the account via the internet. I also took the precaution of making you eighteen years old for the bank's files."

"That's amazing, all by just talking to other computers!"

"Once I'd made a few connections it was easy."

"Looks like you're in business kid," drawled the robot.

"What business is 'e in?" squeaked the marble.

"The mind your own business," said the shark.

"Hey," said Mister Potato Head, "that sounds like a good business to be in."

"So now," said Jim, "you could use your connections

to find my dad?"

"I've been thinking about that," said the mobile, "and I do have one clue as it happens."

All eyes settled on the mobile.

"Er...did your dad ever mention Devon?"

"Devon?" said Jim, his gaze moving from one object in the room to another, as if something might remind him.

"Devon? Isn't that in Cornwall?" asked the robot.

"Yes, where all the walls are made from corn," the marble told the potato. "You know – the way they make fingers from fish, and horses from clothes."

"And drumsticks from chickens," called a smelly trainer.

"Hey," said the shark, "that's nothing. I heard they can make motor cars from meat!"

The little marble crinkled its beady eyes. "Cars made from meat?"

"Sausage Rolls," the shark said with a goofy look.

The mobile beeped for attention. "Jim, did you ever go on holiday to Devon?"

"We might have, when I was little."

"How little was he?" the pterodactyl asked the stealth bomber.

"Too small to see without the aid of a bowl of Cheerios," said the bomber.

"Wow!" said the pterodactyl, so shocked the sock almost fell off its head.

"The reason why I ask about Devon," said the mobile, "is because when I spoke to the bank's computers, I discovered the money was moved through a number of accounts in different names before eventually being transferred to the account of a certain Mr. Ronald Parkin, who at the time lived in a town called Sidmouth - in Devon. It's my guess that your dad used the name Ronald Parkin, but that was two years ago."

Jim gazed out of the window for long moments, thinking. Nobody spoke. Then he looked at the mobile having made up his mind.

"I want to go to Devon to find him," he said.

The mobile snorted. "I'm way ahead of you Jim. The money in your new account means I can use the internet to arrange travel and a place to stay. Better still, we can put a picture of your dad on the net. If anyone knows where he is, they can contact me. Easy-peasy."

12

A banana for a nose.

"How do we put a picture on the internet?" Jim asked the mobile.

"Well first we need a scanner to copy your photo of him."

The marble looked dangerously at the robot. "A scanner!" it whispered, as if repeating a secret word.

"A scanner!?" said the potato, suddenly terrified without knowing why.

"Yes, a SCANNER!" the robot said menacingly right into the potato's plastic ear.

Then the robot frowned at the marble. "What's a scanner?"

"I don't know," squeaked the marble. "I thought you knew."

"A scanner is just a camera," the mobile enlightened them.

The marble, the robot, and especially the potato, all looked relieved. The tiny Frankenstein's monster just burped.

"Unlike modern phones I haven't got a camera built

into me, but that doesn't matter because we should be able to use a scanner in a local library. Jim's dad's picture will then go on the web page that I just this minute created."

The mobile then went online and showed one complex screen of messages after another for perhaps twenty seconds while Jim could only watch and wait. Presently its tiny display cleared and the mobile looked pleased with itself.

"Well that's all taken care of," it said. "We can leave for Devon as soon as your new bank card and PIN arrive."

"Ooh goody!" squealed the marble, suddenly excited. "I'll go and pack my case. Will I need a bikini? Do they have crocodiles in Devon?"

"I think they have crabs," said Jim, without knowing how he knew.

"What are crabs?" asked the potato.

"They're crunchy wriggly things that get stuck between your teeth," said Rupert the shark.

"A bit like small children do," said the pterodactyl.

"I heard they make nice sandwiches" said the lava lamp, its red blobs suddenly agitated.

"What's a nice?" the potato asked.

"It's what crabs make sandwiches with, fool," said the robot. "Don't you listen?"

"I keep telling you it's not my fault," said the potato miserably, "it's my eyes."

"It's your brain you mean," said the shark.

"How can it be? I haven't got one."

"We can make one for you," said the marble. "They're a doddle. You just write 'My brain' on a bit of paper, then you eat the paper."

"But I don't really like the taste of paper," said the potato.

"No problem," said the lamp. "You can write 'My brain' on something you like the taste of."

"Excuse me," said the mobile, "but Jim's right - they do have crabs in Devon."

"There you are then," the lamp told the potato. "You could ask a crab to make you a nice sandwich with 'My brain' written on it. Simple."

"And what's more," said the mobile, "they have holiday cottages to rent, and I've just this minute arranged for us to stay in one near Sidmouth, on a quiet part of the Devon coast. From there we can search for more clues about your dad. And before you ask, I got you a train ticket too. You collect it from Paddington Station. It's all taken care of. I've made special arrangements for the money in your bank account to move to a new account that can't be traced by the usual methods. It's in the name of Mister Jim Smith and you travel a lot. You access the money in your new account with an ATM card using cash machines. Your new card and pin number are in the mail right now. You'll just need to intercept them before your mum does."

Jim looked worried. "Our postman always calls before I leave for school. I'll have to be waiting by the door when he arrives."

"Well even if you don't, your mum will probably assume the letters for Jim Smith have come to the wrong address. She won't open them, though you better make sure she doesn't hand them straight back."

"He'll have to play it by ear," suggested the robot.

"Is that what you do with letters?" asked the potato.

"Course it is," the marble told him. "You read them with your ears. You should be good at it with ears that big."

"But I don't know how to read."

"Perhaps Jim's mum would lend you her reading glasses," the robot put in, "then you could just lie there and let them read for you."

"Yes," squealed the marble, suddenly enthusiastic, "and she could lend you her walking stick so you wouldn't need to walk anywhere because her stick would do that for you as well!"

"The same thing happened when they invented swimming trunks," the shark told them. "I thought it was the end of the line for me. Luckily people decided it was no fun letting their trunks do all the swimming."

"Yeah," chirped the tiny lock on Jim's secret diary, "and look what happened when they invented hiking boots!"

Everyone paused to think about that until Jim got up from the bed and began opening drawers, trying to decide what he would need for the trip. He stopped and looked at the mobile.

"How am I going to sneak past my mum with a suitcase?"

The lamp exchanged a look with the marble. "Why will his mum have a suitcase? Is she going away?"

"Yeah," demanded the marble and looked at Jim, "Why will your mum - "

"Oh be quiet," snapped the shark. "Mister Potato Head's trying to think."

They all turned to look at the potato.

"I don't think we can be quiet that long," said a smelly trainer.

"I know what to do!" shouted the potato, making them all jump. "Jim can hide inside his suitcase, then have someone call at the house and collect it!"

Astounded silence descended on the room.

After a moment the stealth bomber said, "But what if he's mistaken for Mister Suitcase?"

"Who's Mister Suitcase?" asked the lamp.

"He's a superhero suitcase who can fly, and he carries a magic stick of rhubarb to fight his enemies."

"He's my favourite superhero," cried the potato. "He rescues defenceless vegetables from danger!"

"I never heard of Mister Suitcase," said the shark with a knitted brow.

"Maybe he means Mister Fruitface," said the plug on the lamp, "the man who was born with a banana intead of a nose."

"Is he the one who has prunes for eyes and figgy ears?" inquired the pterodactyl, "and lips made from juicy peach slices?"

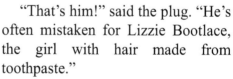 "That's him!" said the plug. "He's often mistaken for Lizzie Bootlace, the girl with hair made from toothpaste."

"And her sister's mum's got a great big bum that's covered in blisters," said the robot to join in the rhyming.

"How did her sister's mum's bum get covered in blisters?" asked the lamp.

"Somebody put hot chestnuts down her pants."

"Er, if I might interrupt," the mobile interrupted,

"Jim doesn't need a suitcase – he won't be taking much with him. Besides, he can draw money from a cash machine for anything else he needs."

So that was it. Between them, Jim and the mobile decided they should leave as soon as the bank card and security PIN number arrived. Jim would greet the postman at the front gate, just to be on the safe side, and pocket the envelopes at once.

His mum probably wouldn't even notice, she'd be too busy worrying about whether the new security system would work properly. It had worked alright for the past few days, so there was no reason why it shouldn't go on working. But technophobes - like other phobes - are not guided by common sense.

13
Doctor, I've caught a bus.

Today was Thursday. Jim was all ready for school as usual, waiting for his mum to find her watch, or her handbag, or a dozen other things that she could misplace. Whatever it was, it would be right there under her nose.

"Jim, I've lost my mouth," she'd say.

"It's right there under your nose," Jim would answer. (That was the little joke that Jim amused himself with at times like this.)

From the corner of his eye he caught sight of the postman and suddenly remembered the imminent arrival of his new PIN number.

"Jim, get the mail will you. I can't find my legs…"

The postman smiled and handed him the only delivery for number forty-seven that day. It was one of those special non-see-through envelopes addressed to the mysterious Mr. J. Smith, the invisible man.

Jim's new ATM card had arrived the day before, and as then, this envelope went directly into his talkative schoolbag – the one with the zipper for a mouth that allowed Jim to silence the bag whenever it became too cheeky, which was quite often.

"Oy," it complained, "that's another letter for Mr. J. Smith. What are you doing with it?"

"I'm pretending to be somebody else," said Jim.

"What!" fulminated the bag. "But that's illegal! Did you know you could be sent to Devil's Island for impersonation?"

"Oh, so now there's an island where you're sent just for the crime of impersonation is there?" piped up the biro sticking out of the bag.

Jim zipped the bag shut; it seemed the easiest solution in the circumstances.

It was not a good day at school. All Jim could think about was leaving home that evening, and he was worried. If not for the one small thought that his dad was out there somewhere, Jim simply would not have contemplated so reckless and dangerous a plan.

When his mum picked him up, he sat beside her listening to the gear-lever knob chatting to the handbrake about what they'd do if they were sent for scrap. His thoughts were miles away in Devon, a place he didn't know and yet would probably be sleeping in that very night, in a strange cottage, alone except for his dad's old mobile. Even with the mobile for company it was still going to be really -

"Jim, I said are you going to get out, or shall I leave you in the car?"

They were home. Home! He went straight up to his room and fell face-down on his bed, trying to imagine what the journey to Devon would be like, picturing himself creeping out of the house in darkness, without even a suitcase. All that he'd take with him would be packed into his schoolbag.

He rolled over on the bed and reached down for the bag, opened it and took out the mobile, his new PIN number letter and the ATM card.

The mobile looked up at him, smiled and said, "All set?"

Jim took a deep breath and sighed. "Not really."

"Having second thoughts is he?" asked the robot.

"I'm just worried that we might get lost," said Jim. "I haven't been to Paddington Station before."

"Well if that bear could do it, you should be alright with a clever mobile phone for company," the pterodactyl said from overhead.

"What bear?" asked the marble in its squeaky voice.

"Waterloo Bear," said the tiny Frankenstein's monster.

It was seven o'clock. Jim had finished his dinner in silence and gone back up to his room, leaving his mum and Lucinda to enjoy their usual helping of Coronation Street. Jim's bag was packed and waiting. All he had in it was an apple, his toothbrush, some clean underpants, the mobile's charger, and his bank card.

"I think the most sensible course of action would be to leave immediately," the mobile told him, sensing Jim's mood and adopting a calm attitude. "Simply pick up your bag – and me of course – walk down the stairs quietly while the coast is clear, slip out by the front door, and catch the first bus to Paddington."

"I caught a bus once," said the schoolbag. "Nothing serious. Just a number 24. I soon recovered."

"Didn't the doctor give you anything for it?" asked

77

one of the smelly trainers.

"He advised me to take a taxi every half hour and go home to bed."

"Before I catch the bus," Jim said, "I need to go to the machine in the high street so I can get some money out."

The mobile looked pleased. "See? You know the drill. This is going to be plain sailing."

Jim looked down at his shoes and pictured them on the bus, getting off at Paddington, walking into the station and getting on a train to Devon.

"Ok," the mobile told him in a firm voice, "now pick up that bag and let's go."

Jim paused for a moment longer, then he fished the note from his pocket that he'd written for his mum and propped it against the lava lamp whose luminous red blobs cast their rosy light on the marble, the robot and Mister Potato Head. They exchanged knowing looks – except for the potato, who looked so sorry for himself that Jim's last job before leaving was to rearrange his eyes.

"Where do you want them?" Jim asked him.

"Ooh, er...I don't know," said the potato.

"Put them on the ends of his fingers," said the robot, "then he can see how he feels."

"Or how about," said a smelly trainer, "sticking one in each side of his head, so he can look both ways at once when he crosses the road."

"I think the best place to have eyes," said Jim, having made his decision, "is where they face the same way you do."

He pressed the eyes into the potato accordingly and

set the vegetable on its plastic feet facing the marble and the robot, right beside his mum's note.

"Ooh look," said the potato. "Somebody left me a letter! What does it say?"

The robot leaned close to the letter and listened. "Nothing."

The potato looked disappointed. "My first ever letter and it's not saying anything."

"If I were you," the lamp suggested, "I'd try talking to it. It might be shy and just waiting for you to make the first move."

The potato turned to the letter. "Hello," he said. "Anybody in?"

"Perhaps it's all written in silent lettering," said Rupert the shark. "You know – like the 'g' in cough, and the 'u' in quack."

"Yeah, and don't forget the silent peas in pea soup," squeaked the little marble.

"Peas always talk to me," said the potato. "I've had some very interesting conversations with them."

"There can't be any peas in this letter then," said the lamp.

"Or bees," said the pterodactyl, "otherwise we'd hear them buzzing."

Jim decided this was a good moment to leave, and tip-toed quietly from the room with a last brief look around. In that instant he comforted himself with the thought that he'd find his dad and everything would be alright.

At the top of the darkened stairway, the wooden knob on the banister wished him a good evening. The stair halfway down creaked just enough to remind Jim to be even more careful. He stopped in the hallway by the front door and listened, as if waiting for a signal to go. A car went by outside, its lights twinkling across the frosted glass in the front door, then all was dark and silent again. Jim opened the door, stepped out and closed it quietly behind him. He swung his bag over his shoulder and, with a determined sniff, set off on his journey to find his dad.

Of course he knew that the moment his mum discovered he was gone, she'd call the police and they'd alert everyone to be on the lookout for a boy fitting his description. That was why the mysterious Mister Jim Smith had had his rail ticket sent to his home address, courtesy of the internet, instead of buying it at the station. People would remember a small boy buying a ticket, but perhaps not a small boy mingling with the crowds before slipping unnoticed onto the train heading to Devon.

First he stopped off at a local cashpoint, withdrew twenty pounds using his new card, and boarded the first bus into central London. Once there, it was a simple enough job for the mobile to locate another bus going to Paddington using an online travel information service.

14

A baby elephant swimming in custard.

So far so good. He'd arrived at Paddington Station. Now he had to get onto the right platform for the Devon train without drawing attention to himself.

The mobile reminded him of the closed circuit TV cameras, high up on the walls; these would be checked later for any sign of a boy on his own.

Although there were not that many passengers travelling to the South West at this time of day, Jim managed to 'attach' himself to a man and a woman, keeping as close to them as he dare without them noticing as they showed their tickets and walked onto the platform.

As soon as the train's automatic doors hissed shut behind him, Jim headed straight for the lavatory and locked himself in to wait until the train left the station. Then he decided that the most inconspicuous way to travel to Devon would be in the lavatory.

He'd been sitting there chatting with the old mobile for a while before deciding to try and sleep a bit. The steady movement of the train and the excitement of their journey had left him feeling exhausted. Turning the mobile off to conserve battery power, he wondered what the cottage it had booked for him would be like. Would it have a comfortable bed?

He thought about his own bed at home and half wished he were there right now. How much nicer that would be than sitting here on a lavatory seat, holding onto the rail to keep from slipping off...

...and then he awoke with a bump and found he had done just that, landing painfully between the lavatory and the wash basin.

"Been at the wine gums have we sir?" ventured a small screw on the basin. "The red ones have the worst effects – especially at high altitudes."

"Better strap yourself in sir," said the flush handle. "We'll be taking off any time now."

"But this is a train," said Jim.

The screw looked at the handle knowingly. "Must've eaten a whole packet."

The train was still moving so Jim decided to open the lavatory door and see where they were, but it was too dark beyond the window to see anything at all. Not even a sky. It was as if someone had painted the outside of the window black.

"They're just changing the film over now sir," a window catch told him briskly. "The second half will start in a tick."

"What film?" said Jim, frowning.

"The one showing at this window, starring fields of cows, a village or two, new housing estates and, I believe, a small sewage treatment works. I admit it's not very exciting, but you could try the screen on the other side of the train. They're showing a Batman movie."

When Jim checked the rest of the carriage he was surprised and a little bit pleased to find it completely empty. After walking its full length and peering cautiously through the connecting doors, he discovered there was no one in the adjoining carriages either. He didn't know if he should be worried by this fact.

Then he noticed how comfortable the seats looked, and wondered if it would be safe to stay here; he could always go back into hiding when they reached a station. So he dropped his bag on the seat and flopped down, immediately deciding it was the right choice.

"What's that you've got there then my young traveller?"

Jim looked around to see who was talking in the empty carriage.

"Go on, show us it," prompted a second voice.

"Looks like a thingummy whatsit," said a third voice.

"Nah, it's a gadget," said another voice.

"I reckon it's a gizmo," said another.

Each time Jim tried to locate one voice, it fell silent and another began somewhere else. Then he noticed a movement at the spherical end of a long silvery handrail where two bolts like eyes stared back at him.

"What you lookin' at?" the handrail demanded, more from embarrassment than rudeness.

"Did you call this a gizmo?" asked Jim, waggling the mobile.

"Who, me?" said the handrail sheepishly.

"It was 'im," accused the identical rail opposite. "Me, I think it looks more like a thingummy whatsit."

"Ok, so what is a thingummy whatsit then?" asked

the seat next to Jim.

"They used to roam the earth before real words existed," said the red door-release button knowledgeably.

The handrails seemed impressed.

"In the very beginning," the door button went on, "little bits of words swam free in the seas..."

"Do you mean the letters that words are made from?" said Jim.

"Exactly. We call them letters now, but in those early days when the ocean was a great big alphabet soup, they didn't have a name."

"So what happened?" asked the seat, enthralled.

"Some of those primitive letters crawled onto dry land and eventually grew into the words we use today."

"What, like grobblychops?" asked the seat.

"Oh no, that one went extinct very early on, along with snilth, drusset, trenge and others like them. Archaeographers are always digging up fossilised word bones and mistaking fragments of a prehistoric p for an early b or a d."

"Never mind that," the first handrail eyed the mobile, "is it a gizmo or a gadget 'e's 'olding?"

"It's obviously a gadget you drainpipe!" announced the second rail.

"A gizmo is a gadget, you tubular bell!" contradicted the first rail.

"'Ow can a gizmo be a gadget?" contended the second rail. "They don't even sound the same?!"

"Well..." interrupted Jim, "...a bunny is a rabbit, but they don't sound the same either."

"Alright mister clever socks," challenged the second

handrail, "so what do they sound like?"

"Like a baby elephant swimming in custard?" suggested the first handrail.

"Or a gale blowing through your pyjama bottoms," tried the seat.

"Or the sound that bats make when they smell a ripe turnip," piped up the biro in Jim's schoolbag.

"Erm, I don't think rabbits sound like anything at all," said Jim.

"You mean they sound like nothing?" said the seat. "What does nothing sound like?"

"I don't know," complained the first handrail, "but it's all I ever seem to do."

"You can eat as much as you like though and never get full!" said the other handrail.

15

Suck a sprout.

A SPROUT

"I suggest you both get a grip of yourself," the red door-release button told the two rails. Then to Jim: "Just ignore these idiots. They're so stupid they think the train moves while everything else stays still. You must have seen the world in your travels – tell them the train stays still while everything else moves."

Jim looked uncertain.

"Just look out of the window," the door button went on, "and you can see with your own eyes. Everything outside is whizzing past, but we're stationary!"

"It's true," the seat told Jim. "I'm a little pencil, he's a sheet of writing paper, and you're a packet of envelopes!"

"Never mind him," the door button said to Jim, "why don't you show us that whatever-it-is you're holding and put us out of our misery?"

"Yeah, and tell us where you're headed," said the first rail.

"Any why," said the second rail.

"And why not," chirped the seat. "We want to know everything."

"I'm looking for my dad," Jim told them. He regarded the ancient mobile morosely. "This is my dad's old mobile phone."

"What's a dad?" asked the first rail.

"He's somebody I used to know. He went out one day and didn't come home."

"P'raps he got on the wrong train," said the seat.

Then, before anyone could say another word, all the lights winked out together, plunging their little world into complete darkness.

"Hang on everybody!" yelled the 1st handrail.

"Hang onto yourself!" cried his opposite number.

"Lie down and brace yourself," the seat next to Jim warned.

"System failure, system failure!" shrieked the door button, its luminous face blinking red in the blackness.

Panic gripped the compartment's parts.

"Hey, Red, what's the news?" called the seat nervously across the dark compartment.

"Where's everything gone?" screamed the 2nd rail.

"I've been struck blind!" cried the 1st rail.

"Pity it wasn't dumb," the 2nd rail said before renewing its cries.

"Help me!" called the 1st rail.

"No, help me!" echoed the 2nd rail.

"Is this the end of the line for us?" said the seat beside Jim.

Then the lights came on again to wails of relief.

"Well that's alright then," the red door button

told them all. "I bet they only turned the lights off to frighten us. They have to do that occasionally - it's in the manual."

"How'd you know it's in the manual?" asked the 1st rail.

"I saw a copy at the factory when they were building me into the carriage, but I could only read a few words because I didn't have my glasses with me."

"What, your bird impersonating glasses?" asked the seat, suddenly interested.

"Don't be daft," replied the door button. "Who'd wear their bird impersonating glasses in a train building factory?"

"No, wait a moment," interrupted the 1st rail. "I've heard that train factories are overrun by grannets and pelingtons; just the thought of a train factory is enough to bring the taste of fish to a seabird's beak."

"Well you've been sadly misinformed," the door button said. "The only wildlife I ever saw in that factory was a tame toilet-roll that somebody brought in to keep them company."

"How'd you know it wasn't a wild one?" asked the first rail.

"If you whistled it would come and sit on your shoulder large as life," said the door button. "Really friendly it was."

The train began to decelerate just then, and Jim pressed his nose against the window waiting for the station sign to slide into view, which it did a few seconds later. His stomach jumped; it read Sidmouth.

Immediately he activated the mobile to inform it and reached for his bag, then he was heading for the nearest door, bidding his fellow travellers goodbye and receiving comments such as: "Don't do anything we would," and "When in doubt, suck a sprout."

"Wait a moment," the mobile warned as Jim reached out to press the red door button. "We can't just walk through the barrier in plain view of everyone. This has to be done covertly."

"What does covertly mean?" Jim asked as the waiting room crawled past, the train about to stop.

"It means we stay out of sight," said the mobile. "Let's go back along the carriage and use the door furthest from the ticket barrier."

Crouching low, Jim hurried towards the rear of the train. Outside he could see a short, deserted platform and beyond that the lights of houses. As the train lurched to a halt he hit the nearest door button and the door hissed aside.

"Careful!" cautioned the mobile. "Jump off and walk away from the barrier. Look for another way out. See? Over there – the car park. Go that way. Quickly!"

16
A funny looking cow.

"'Ere, where you goin?" demanded a white fence post as he passed.

"'Ere, where you goin?" demanded the next post.

"'Ere, where you goin?" demanded the next one.

Jim had to pass this same inquiry from each of the fence posts until he reached the end of the fence, where he was able to walk straight into the small car park; it was mostly in darkness because there was only one overhead light.

"And where's your car then?" demanded the pay-and-display ticket machine.

"Er...it won't start," Jim fibbed to the machine, "so I've decided to walk home."

"Oh well, that's different sir," said the machine. "I'd offer you a lift home in my Mercedes only the missis threatened me with a shepherd's pie this evening, and as that's my favourite, well, you understand sir..."

Jim thought for a moment. "Have you really got a Mercedes?"

The machine would have blushed had it been human. "No I 'aven't, but it's the thought that counts, am I right sir?"

"Come on," urged the mobile. "It's over a mile to the cottage, and it's all on foot."

"If you're walkin', the best way is definitely on foot sir," said the machine. "A wise choice. Good night to you now."

"Goodnight," Jim said, and waited until he was out of the car park before consulting the mobile about their route. It seemed their cottage was actually about two miles distant. That was a lot further than Jim had ever walked before in one go. Not that two miles meant anything to him; it was only a number.

The mobile had their route all planned and supplied Jim with step by step directions as they went along. All Jim had to concern himself with – apart from a long walk in the dark – was staying out of sight. A boy walking along pitch black country roads late at night might be reported to the police, and that would be the end of Jim's daring little escapade.

Thankfully there were few vehicles about, but whenever one appeared Jim crouched under the hedgerow until its lights swept past.

Eventually he left the country road and found himself on a narrow lane that wound steeply upward before bending sharply to the right. This was where Jim fell into the river. Well, not a river exactly; it was more like a quietly trickling stream, but in the dark a stream could easily be a river.

"Oy, 'oo you pushin?!" said a small voice.

"Mind me tendrils!" said another.

"Who let that bull out?" came a third.

Many small, reedy voices screeched together in the darkness, and when Jim got to his feet there was water in his trainers that squelched interestingly with each step. He imagined it was a bit like walking on frogs.

Now he edged his way along the side of the dark lane, occasionally bending down to touch the old tarmac surface to make sure he didn't plunge into another river, wishing he'd brought his torch. When he stopped and listened, he could hear only his own breath as the blackness pressed in on him.

Somewhere close by a cow bellowed, just once. Then something rustled at his feet. He looked down at the sound. It couldn't be a cow, unless it was a very small one.

"Are you a cow?" he said quietly in the darkness.

"Don't know," replied a furry little voice. "I was never told."

It was probably a mouse or something like it. The rustling moved away and grew fainter, then stopped. Another cow coughed.

"Perhaps it was a cow after all," Jim said to cheer himself up, because now he was thinking about his mum, knowing she'd have found his note and called the police. She'd be worried, but at least she'd know this had been his idea; it wasn't as if he'd been kidnapped.

Then he remembered the unpleasant man who'd threatened to see him later. Well, he couldn't find him here in Devon; to Jim this seemed like the most secret place on earth. Even Jim didn't know where he was.

He fished the mobile out of his bag and keyed it into life so its tiny screen lit up like a tiny TV in a huge dark room.

"Everything ok?" it asked.

"Well, I just fell into a river and my feet are soaked.

A funny looking cow.

I can't see anything. I don't know where we are. Where are we?"

A tiny map appeared on the glowing display but there wasn't enough detail on it. What's more, the directions he'd been sent in the post for finding the cottage were useless in the dark, and it was no good trying to read them by the mobile's light, which was much too dim for that.

Between them, Jim and the mobile came to the conclusion that somewhere along this little lane was the even narrower track that led to their cottage, and it would be somewhere on the left.

"Why did we pick this place?" Jim asked.

"Because it's so secluded," answered the mobile. "Besides, they don't expect people to find it in the dark after walking from Sidmouth. A car would be the usual way to arrive, and cars have lights."

Jim sighed and set off walking again, wondering how he'd find a track when he couldn't even see his own feet. His legs ached and he was hungry. He'd been peering into the dark for so long, it felt as though someone had glued his eyes open.

After what seemed like an age, he imagined he could make out a gap in the trees.

"I think there's an opening just here," he said, inching forward until gravel sounded under his shoes. Then he saw the shape of a building. He managed to locate the front door and the plant pot nearby with the key underneath it. To his relief the key slid smoothly into the lock. Then they were inside, finally.

17

A good night's sleep.

"Lights," Jim called out in the dark cottage. Nothing happened.

"You'll be lucky," said the mobile. "I doubt there's voice-activation circuitry in an old place like this."

"It may be old," said a small voice with a West-country accent, "but we like it right enough. And who might you be when you're at home?"

Jim's fingers groped for a light switch and found it activated a matching pair of shaded bulbs on the opposite pink wall that bulged in strange places. It was like being inside a giant blancmange.

"I'm Jim. I've rented the cottage." He looked around for the owner of the voice yet saw no obvious source.

This was very different from home. The first thing he noticed was the smell of dampness. There were huge black wooden beams holding up the ceiling, a great big sunken fireplace occupied one entire wall, and on the opposite wall were two small windows with tiny glass panes. The only furniture was a massive old sofa piled high with cushions, and a table fashioned from a wooden barrel.

"Well, don't just stand there like a garden gnome. Come in and warm the place up."

It was the barrel that had spoken; it had a jovial voice with a nature to match.

"Ignore the bats and badgers – they're friendly enough if you don't mind your nose being nibbled in the night," warned the copper warming pan that hung on the wall beside the fireplace.

"Or getting' scared out of your wits by the ghost of the mad old woodcutter who 'anged himself upstairs," chimed the grandmother clock.

"By 'is ears," added the coal scuttle on the hearth.

"I thought 'e chopped 'is own 'ead off?" said the brass-handled fire iron.

"No, no. That were Jethro the poacher – fell into the trap 'e'd set for the postman."

"People don't set traps for the postman," said Jim.

"Oh-ho, another misguided tourist!" laughed the warming pan. "You lot don't know the 'arf of what goes on down 'ere at the dead of night."

"Specially on darkest Dartmoor!" chimed the grandmother clock.

"At the full 'o the moon," spouted a large black kettle that stood on a ledge set into the fireplace. "And there's probably such a moon tonight, so you best get that fire goin'!"

"I think I'd like a cup of tea and something to eat first," said Jim.

"Well then, get yourself into the back kitchen

there," said a Toby jug from its niche in the fireplace. "My missis has been waitin' all day for you to turn up. Thought you'd got yerself lost we did."

"Or recruited by Morris Dancers," said the kettle.

"An' it's quite a stroke o' luck you weren't savaged by a herd of wanderin' lettuces," added the warming pan.

"It's right that is," confirmed a plump cushion on the lumpy sofa. "They go around on black stilts so you can't see 'em, but worst of all, they're in cahoots with very badly behaved pomegranates."

"Even if you missed the wanted posters," said a log on the hearth, "you must've 'eard a few screams."

"Then we wondered if you'd gone to the wrong 'ouse," chipped in a small footstool that sat next to a row of ancient horse-brasses strung on a black leather belt.

"What's the wrong house?" asked Jim.

"Most of our visitors go to the wrong 'ouse before they arrives," added a brass handled fire-iron, nodding wisely and winking. "Then they rolls up 'ere all red faced an' silly like."

Jim was confused.

"Ha-hargh!" chortled one of the horse brasses right beside Jim's ear, making him jump. "They means the local hostelry, boy."

"Hostelry?" said Jim.

"The pub boy! It's called The Wrong 'Ouse!"

"But most of our visitors seem to think it's the right house!" said another of the horse brasses.

"'E don't seem the type to go in pubs," observed the footstool.

"Er, I think I'll go into the back kitchen then," said Jim, and he left his bag and the mobile on the sofa, backed out through the other door in the room, and discovered it opened onto a tiny lobby with three other doors, each of which bore a ceramic plate with a little picture painted on it. One plate had a small image of a tombstone with the word 'Kitchen' carved on it. Another showed a green-faced corpse lying in a coffin beside the word 'Bedroom'. The third picture was of a hangman's noose, and the words 'Back door'.

"So where d'you want to be then?" asked the bedroom door sign, looking Jim up and down quizzically.

"The kitchen please," Jim answered. "I want something to eat."

"You quite sure you don't want to go up to bed?" called the warming pan, "though you best ignore the free-range scones – they often fly in through the bedroom window at night lookin' for a place to roost."

"Take no notice of him," said the sign. "The bedroom is rather nicely decorated, and there's a dinky little bathroom next to it. Pity about the previous tenants, but never you mind about them."

"Pigs they were," said the back door sign.

"Who?" asked Jim. "The previous tenants?"

"'S'right," replied the door sign. "Mister and Missis Pig was their name."

"No, no, 't'weren't Pig, it were Big. Mister and Missis Big," the kitchen door sign corrected the back door sign.

"You mean to say," interjected the back door sign, "that the Pigs were Big?"

"That's right," said the kitchen door sign. "They were big pigs! Ah-hahahggghhh!" The sign laughed the way only a door sign can.

Jim turned the old wrought-iron handle on the kitchen door and went into a very, very small room with one tiny window, a midget cooker, a teeny-weeny sink with one cold tap, and a minuscule fridge. Everything else was in proportion to these, including a dainty little yellow and white teapot – one cup capacity only – that brightened the instant Jim switched on the light.

18

Cover yourself in margarine.

"Ah, come in, come in me dear," said the teapot, its roundly rosy cheeks blossoming pinkly. "I'm all ready to do you a pot of tea. The cups are over the sink – or should I say the sink's under the cups. The water's in the tap - well, not in the tap exactly, it's in the mice that carry the water to the tap. And my old man Toby in the other room will be waitin' to warm 'is whiskers by the fire – when you've lit it that is."

"I never lit a fire before," Jim told the tiny teapot. "And that's a really big one. How do I do it?"

"Oh, don't you worry yourself over that. My old man Toby will instruct you. 'E's never lit a fire either, but 'e's sat around and watched many a townie make a proper donkey's backside of it. That's 'is 'obby, see, watchin' people 'oo think they're clever make a donkey's bum of theirselves."

Jim filled the kettle and boiled the water on the cooker, made the tea, and found to his delight that the fridge was stocked with eggs, milk, cheese, clotted cream and fresh vegetables, and taking pride of place on the top shelf were...

"Sausages!"

"Bless you," said the little teapot.

"Those are my favourites," said Jim. They were the kind that had bits of green – herbs - showing through the skin.

Jim took his tea into the other room. "They're like big pink fingers," he told the mobile, "except for the green bits."

"I 'ad a cousin with fingers like that," said the footstool. "Trouble was, 'e 'ad legs to match, poor love. All his children were the same. Sold 'em to a travellin' pumpkin smuggler 'e did."

"We do lots of local specialities like them sausages 'ere in Devon," said the old barrel. "Most are house trained but some can leave an unpleasant surprise in your wellies."

"Your dad liked sausages I seem to recall," said the mobile. "He used to order them specially from a famous sausage shop in this part of the world."

Jim looked interested. "That's another clue my dad's here somewhere."

"I imagine that sausages make very good clues," the barrel told them hollowly.

"Yes," agreed the warming pan. "You could leave 'em lyin' around and folks would find 'em and say, 'Ah-ha! Another clue'."

"But another clue to what?" said Jim.

"To the fact," the barrel said, "that you've found a sausage!"

"I suggest you take everything old George says with a pinch of salt lad," the kettle on the hearth said. "'E used to be filled with rum and 'e's a bit, well, let's just say unreliable."

"Ar, that's right," agreed George the barrel happily. "I'm fine first thing in the mornings, but by lunchtime I starts to feel a bit groggy."

"'E's 'armless though," the brass-handled fire iron assured Jim. "Wouldn't 'urt a fly."

"Phew, that's a relief," squeaked the fly that had settled on the barrel.

"So what's all this about you lookin' for your dad then?" piped up the small footstool.

"'E can tell us all about that when 'e's made up the fire, am I right?" said the Toby jug, twitching its bushy whiskers. "'Bout time we 'ad a bit of 'eat in the place. Go on lad, there's plenty of logs by the door, and matches are in the kitchen – my missis will show you where."

"Remember to cover yourself in margarine as well," said the warming pan, "just in case."

"An' you better jump up and down a few times while readin' the back of an open cornflakes packet," said the old barrel.

"What for?" said Jim, frowning.

"'Cos then you'll get cornflakes all over the floor," said the barrel, "an' there'll be a lovely crunchin' noise when somebody walks on 'em!"

The horse-brasses twinkled in anticipation of a nice big fire burning in the inglenook. The idea appealed to Jim too.

He began by rolling up newspaper and putting it in the grate. Some pieces of kindling showed him how to build them over the paper in the shape of a tent, and a small log suggested that he stick two firelighters inside the paper tent. That done, he took a match from a big box and lit the bonfire, then stood back to watch as the flames began creeping upward.

The warming pan gazed fondly on the scene, its eyes reflecting miniature versions of the flames as bits of kindling crackled and threw off tiny sparks. The horse brasses, now silent, snuggled against their black leather belt, while the barrel rocked gently from side to side as if recalling its rum-filled past.

All the room's occupants seemed to mellow as the fire grew – except for the large black kettle, which didn't like the heat. It turned its back and dozed in the corner of the hearth behind the logs that Jim had thoughtfully placed to shield it.

Half an hour later, with a good blaze curling up from the logs and a pan of sausages sizzling on the little cooker in the kitchen, Jim told the cottage's motley inhabitants about his dad, the money, the two men, and everything. He introduced the mobile, which then amazed the locals with its explanation of computers and voice-activated circuitry, the internet and the world wide web.

They'd all seen mobile phones at the cottage before, but none had ever spoken to them.

Jim, now settled on the plump sofa with his plate of delicious if somewhat burned sausages, would have been just as interested as the rest had he not been so tired. The blazing logs had brought a rosy glow to his cheeks to match the little teapot's.

When the Toby jug yawned, it seemed like a signal for them all to call it a night. Jim put a wire-mesh guard in front of the dwindling fire, turned off the lights and went up to the bedroom to find a double bed with an oversized quilt that bulged in funny places as if filled with strangely shaped objects. It was made from unusual material too. Sewn together were squares of shaggy pink carpet, three legs from a pair of moth-nibbled moleskin trousers, a threadbare skull and crossbones pirate flag, a smelly piece of brown buffalo hide, and that long lost section from the Bayeux Tapestry depicting an English soldier falling off his bike.

Jim decided that it would be really cosy to take the quilt down to the living room and curl up under it on the sofa by the fire. And that was just what he did, though tired as he was, he lay for a while staring at the dying embers before falling asleep and dreaming that he was sharing a bed with giant buffalo hide dumplings.

19

Join me in a pork pie.

When Jim woke next morning the cottage was surrounded by a thick mist and seemed to be wrapped in a ball of cotton wool. The room was cold even though embers still glowed dimly in the fireplace.

"Ar, so you're up then?" said the barrel, yawning. "It's still a bit early for me - I likes to sleep in of a Sunday."

Jim was about to inform the barrel that today was Saturday when the big black kettle puffed its lid at him, touched its head and pointed meaningfully at the barrel.

Jim understood. To the Toby jug he said, "Will Mrs. Teapot be up yet if I want to make a cup of tea?"

"Will she be up?! I'll say. She'll 'ave the sheep shorn, the ducks' bills paid in full and a new 'ousing estate built I wouldn't be at all surprised. Oh-ho yes. But you go on in anyhow."

Through the window of the tiny cramped kitchen Jim was pleased to see the mist clearing to reveal patches of blue sky, and his first view of the rear garden:

a small square of lawn in the middle of which was a sculpture of a brontosaurus made from old bicycles and garden tools, and painted pink. Surrounding that was a little crazy-paved path and fruit trees, their buds well formed by this time of year. Just beyond the fruit trees a dense wall of grass lead on to wild blackberry bushes and a thicket of gorse. The garden appeared to merge with the surrounding countryside.

"Tea is it?" sang the tiny teapot. "I'm all yours m'dear."

Jim even found cornflakes in a minute cupboard, but felt guilty eating breakfast before he'd washed his face. He forgot that he'd slept on a sofa in his clothes and shoes, and not even brushed his teeth before going to sleep.

"I expect my mum's worried," he told the little teapot, his mouth full of cornflakes. "She thinks I'm hopeless at looking after myself."

"I expect all mums are like that," the little teapot told him in its musical voice. "They 'ave to be – little boys are little men, and we all know 'ow 'opeless men are when it comes to bein' tidy, makin' tasty broth from their old socks an' seein' the cat's nicely shaved."

Jim put his bowl down so he had a hand free to wipe the tear off his cheek. "It's not fair," he said in a wobbly voice. "I used to have a mum and a dad, and now I haven't got either of them."

"'Course you 'ave," scolded the teapot gently. "You've still got 'em. They're just not 'ere that's all."

But Jim wouldn't be comforted. "I wish I wasn't either," he said in a small voice. "I wish I was at home."

"What's 'e doin' that for?" the small fridge asked

the equally small cooker. "Don't do nobody any good, that."

"'Aven't you got any feelings?" asked the cooker.

"Don't think so, no. I'm a fridge."

"Yes you do," the little sink contradicted. "You 'ave cold feelings."

"Does that mean I'm a bad person then?" the fridge asked innocently.

"Well," considered the sink, "it would, if you were a person. But as you're just a fridge I s'pose it's alright."

"What about me then?" asked the cooker. "I 'ave 'ot feelings. What does that make me?"

"A pretty useless fridge!" squeaked the single brass tap over the sink.

"Be quiet all of you," commanded the little teapot. "Can't you see the boy's upset?" To Jim the teapot said, "You're lucky. Gettin' upset just brings a few tears. When I get upset – which isn't very often I admit – I spits tea all over the kitchen floor!"

She smiled shyly at Jim, who couldn't help smiling back.

"Now you run along and find your dad," she said, "and I'll expect you both back 'ere for a nice cup of tea, 'ow's that?"

Jim wandered through to the main room wiping his itchy cheeks, trying to arrange his thoughts into a straight line. He finally decided that now he was here in Devon he ought to go into Sidmouth and look for his dad instead of feeling sorry for himself. He picked up the mobile just for something to do and keyed it into life.

"And what time do you call this?" it said. "We

should be in Sidmouth library scanning your dad's picture for the internet."

"I'd better go and wash my face first," he said. "Mum would only moan at me if I didn't."

"That's what mums do is it?" asked the footstool. "Moan at you for not doin' things?"

"Well, sometimes they moan at you for doing things."

"Mums sound really strange," the barrel decided. "Are they dangerous at all?"

"When they drive cars they are," said Jim.

Shortly afterwards Jim found himself on a path through the nearby wood that led to Sidmouth, guided by the mobile.

"According to the online tourist map," the mobile was saying, "this path runs along the clifftop and descends a steep hill into the town. It's only about half a mile – as the crow flies."

"How far is it if the crow wants to walk?" Jim asked, watching a lone seagull soaring overhead.

"Yeah, answer that one, fig feet!" called the seagull.

"Oh alright," said the mobile, "I admit it's probably twice that, but it's a nice day, and we could be in worse places."

"A pork pie for instance," said a crow in hiking boots going the other way.

They emerged through a gap in the trees onto the coastal path that ran along the clifftop and gave a breathtaking panoramic view of the sea with the sun sparkling on it, stretching away around the coast on either side. Just here the cliffs rose up a hundred feet and more from the shingle beach.

Jim went as close to the edge as he dared and looked down, scared yet exhilarated by the terrifying drop.

"Coo, this is amazing!" he told the terrified schoolbag. "I bet we'd be smashed to little bits if we fell down there."

At that, the schoolbag threw up in a bush.

Just behind Jim a voice said, "Well, are you going to stand around all day or what?"

He turned and saw a wooden bench watching him expectantly.

"I don't mind you sittin' on me," it said. "What I object to is kids walking' on me or folks puttin' their fags out on my arms, or dogs cockin' their legs next to me."

Jim didn't especially want to sit down but felt obliged to now.

"Holidaying are we?" asked the bench conversationally, "or d'you live round these parts? Not seen you before 'ave I?"

"I'm looking for my dad," Jim told the bench. "He might have walked along here. Perhaps you've seen him?"

"What sort of trousers does 'e wear?"

Jim produced his usual frown. "I can't remember."

"'As 'e got a square bottom, round bottom, a giant bottom that overhangs, or one that whistles in the wind?"

"Surely you can't remember all the people who sit on you?" said Jim.

"Who said anything about people? I'm talking about bottoms plain and simple. Bottoms in trousers, bottoms in skirts, and so on. I 'ave 'ad the rare bikini bottom parked on me, but in my line of work you 'ave to be prepared for anything. Take the smooth with the rough so to speak. I never forget any of 'em. The cheekier the better I say."

"We have to go now," Jim told the bench without actually having sat down, "but we'll be coming back this way."

"Bring some sandwiches with you," suggested the bench. "Enjoy the view." It screwed up its face. "Just don't bring any babies in nappies, please. Turns my stomach just thinkin' about it!"

20
Smelly belly jelly

Jim found Sidmouth library easily enough thanks to the mobile. The lady in the library (who reminded Jim of a dead person because of her white face and black lips) showed him to the small computer section which had a printer and scanner. There'd be a small charge, but Jim had drawn more money from a cashpoint, bought himself a bag of nuts and a badge that said 'Babies Suck', and asked if he could be left to do the scanning himself. It seemed that was perfectly normal, even for small boys, most of whom knew more about computers than their parents did.

When the dead library lady had gone Jim took out the mobile. "Ok, I'm ready. What do we do now?"

"Just put the picture of your dad on the scanner and close the lid. I'll do the rest."

"Don't you have to be connected?"

"I already am," said the mobile. "WiFi."

"Why not?" said the scanner start button.

Jim let the mobile get on with it while he kept an eye open for the dead lady. She might have thought it a bit strange that a mobile could operate a scanner by itself.

"Can't I do something?" asked the schoolbag.

"You can keep quiet," Jim told it, and zipped its mouth shut.

"Will this take long," he asked the mobile.

A few seconds later the mobile said, "No, it didn't. I've uploaded the picture. Let's go."

Slightly amazed, Jim retrieved his dad's picture and left the library.

Across the road he noticed a supermarket, and remembering the sausages he'd enjoyed the previous evening he decided to get some more.

Outside the supermarket rows of shopping trolleys waited patiently for drivers. Most were chained up in case they tried to escape, but one had been left to run free.

"Hey kid," it called, "I can help you find your way around the store."

"But I only want - "

"No," said the trolley, "don't tell me – you want a porridge-friendly TV that takes itself for walks, a rechargeable flying toilet-roll holder, time-travelling weetabix that smell of mice, self-inflating all-weather fish sticks, reusable rubber bat biscuits, gift-wrapped smelly belly jelly, and clockwork lobster whistles. Well you're in luck kid - we've got them all!"

Jim took the trolley and pushed it through the automatically opening supermarket door.

"Ok, let's get this show on the road," said the trolley.

"Planning a dinner party? I recommend one of our new ready meals: Free range chicken vests in a deep-fried cat-litter crust and worm custard, presented on a bed of disposable hand-wipes. It's best served piping hot in a pink plastic potty, with a nice bottle of wart remover to wash it all down."

"Have you got any of those sausages with little green specks in them?"

"Well, if you must wear jewellery," said the trolley, "go ahead, but remember to grab yourself a store magazine kid. And hey – better get your passport stamped for the Chinese food section."

As they passed the magazine racks they were assailed with promotional offers:

"FREE in this edition!" a hobby mag called out to Jim. "How to build your own nuclear submarine from slug slime, orange peel and half a cardboard egg-box."

"Want my breastfeeding tips?" offered a mag for new mums.

"Always wean your hamster by candle-light," hailed a pets mag.

"Advice for haemorrhoids sufferers!" said a medical mag.

"Sprinkle compost round the bottom," said a gardening mag.

"Trouble with spots?" called a teen mag.

"Sandpaper first, then a good coat of weatherproof paint," answered a DIY mag.

When the magazines began arguing amongst themselves Jim turned a corner into the fruit and vegetable area.

"Who likes pheasant?" called a tin of Baxter's

scotch broth.

A stripy green watermelon, lounging idly amongst the fruit and vegetables, said, "What the 'eck's a pheasant?"

"Dunno, but there's one in this month's recipe feature," piped up a mango, "as you'd know if you could read, you melon!"

Jim took the store magazine over to the melon and showed it the picture on page 36. "That's a pheasant," he whispered.

The melon wrinkled its nose in disgust. "I can't look at that!" it said, shocked. "I'm a vegetarian!"

"A vegetarian!!!" protested the ranks of potatoes, sprouts and cucumbers.

"Murdering divil!" screamed a spud with an Irish accent.

"Genocide!" hissed a cauliflower.

"Insecticide!" trilled a high-pitched chorus of greenfly on the lettuces.

"Come on, let's get away from these lunatics," said the store mag. "And take my advice, always eat your vegetables with your fingers in your ears."

"And a non-stick frying pan sellotaped to your granny!" a sprout called after them defiantly.

Jim eventually located the sausages with green bits in them and allowed the trolley to guide him to the supermarket exit proudly bearing its solitary passenger.

"I'd rather you didn't chain me to the others," the trolley said when they were outside. "Once you taste freedom there's no going back."

21

A lovely seaweed quiche.

With the sausages stowed away in his schoolbag, Jim sat on a bench on the sea front and was surprised to see his dad's picture on the mobile's tiny screen; the name Ronald Parkin appeared below the picture.

"If anyone out there has information about Mr. Parkin they can simply contact me," said the mobile. "Who knows, your dad himself might even see this."

As Jim watched a gang of gulls squabble over a bright orange wig that one of them had snatched from an elderly lady's head, he tried to remember his dad not as a small photograph but a real, live person. That was when he noticed the hollow feeling in his stomach, and he set off to find some lunch.

"Why not come inside and 'ave a bite to eat and a cup of coffee?" coaxed the wooden sign standing on the pavement outside a little café. "Stuff yourself with our salty seaweed quiche, crab's claws in clotted cream, scones and winkle jam, seagull's beak pasties – we do the lot, an' it's all freshly made by people wearing diver's suits, just to make sure it's nice an' hygienic like."

Jim decided to go further along the lane to a bakery that had cakes in the window. Inside was a glass counter displaying more scones, home made biscuits and buns. Jim's stomach gurgled at the sight.

He bought two giant baps, one filled with tuna and mayonnaise – his favourite - and the other stuffed full of home-made chicken curry. He liked curry but hadn't seen it served in a bun before, though it smelled amazing even from inside the bag. He also liked the look of their thick custard slices and bought two.

The girl in the shop beamed at him over the glass counter. "Bless me, you're never goin' to eat all that yourself?" She had red teeth from sucking a joke sweet someone had given her.

"Bet 'e is," whispered one of the scones on display to its neighbour. "'E looks the sort who'd pig 'imself till 'e burst. Then there'd be a stupendulous explosion and bits of 'is insides would go flyin' in all directions."

"An' bits of 'is outsides," said the other scone.

"Well, I 'ope 'e waits till 'e's out of the shop," commented a cream cake, "or there'll be a terrible mess in 'ere!"

Despite the observation Jim could hardly wait to get back to the talkative bench on the clifftop and tuck into everything. He simply didn't notice the tiny gold ring, or the lip it was attached to, or even the face of the young man they were on who, together with his sidekick, had just stepped out of a pub on the corner of the lane opposite while Jim was busy admiring the contents of his paper bag.

The younger man grabbed his companion's arm and nodded towards Jim. "Am I seeing things or what?"

"What sort of things?" asked his mate.

"Wilson's kid is what!"

The other man followed his gaze and chuckled. "Yeah, it's 'im alright."

"Wonderful things, computers," the younger man said. "You can find anybody anywhere when you know 'ow."

"I don't like 'em much cos they 'urt my knees," said the other man.

"You should get one that you don't have to pedal," said the younger man.

"Come on then, let's get 'im!" said his companion, who was about to cross the road when his colleague stopped him, rolling his eyes.

"Gordon Bennett! We don't want 'im, it's 'is dad we're 'ere for."

"Uh, yeah."

"So we just follow 'im, right?"

The other's eyes narrowed with cunning. "Yeah, right. So what we waitin' for?"

"You to stop bein' a king sized prawn."

They waited until Jim had turned a corner and disappeared from sight before setting off in pursuit.

"I'm right partial to them king sized prawns," said the older man as they tried to hurry without looking suspicious, "'specially with a great big dollop of mushy peas and loads of chips."

"Mushy peas?!" said his friend. "I bet that looks disgustin!"

"Yeah, it does. I 'ave to eat it with me eyes shut or

I'd be sick."

The younger man ignored him, desperate not to let Jim get away, but he needn't have worried, for as they rounded the next corner Jim was just a few yards ahead.

The younger man stopped so suddenly that his partner walked into the back of him.

"Gor, what you doin!?"

"Well you just stopped!"

"Oh, I beg your pardon your majesty! Now come on, but gently does it."

They kept pace with their quarry all the way to the top of the cliff, where it seemed they and Jim were the only people on the coast path. Here the older man stopped to catch his breath and turned back to admire the view.

"Just look at that eh? Nice innit? I might retire to a place like this."

Ahead of him the younger man halted, looking exasperated. "Well why don't we forget all about the kid and find you a nice little place to settle down, alright?"

22

It tastes a bit fishy.

Fifty yards away Jim plonked himself down on the bench he'd talked with earlier and reached into the paper bag, almost able to taste the tuna-filled bap through his fingertips.

"I recognise that bag," said the bench. "Rosa's Bakery if I'm not mistaken. I see a lot of those. In summer you can 'ardly move for 'em up 'ere, blowin' about in the wind like paper seagulls they are. I'd suggest to the Council that they stick a bin beside me, only I don't get into town very often."

Jim pulled the bulging bap from the bag and examined it with great interest as if it was an unidentified flying object he'd just picked up.

"Let's see now," said the bench as Jim put the bag with the other bap down on it, "that feels like another bap on my 'ead. Nice and heavy. I'm guessing there's meat in it, with something like, um, mayonnaise, or, no, wait on a tick...it's one of them curry things innit?"

"That's fantastic!" said Jim with a big mouthful of tuna bap, spitting bits of it everywhere.

"Oh deary me," the bench went on, suddenly

alarmed, "don't tell me you bought a custard slice as well!?"

Jim stopped mid-chew and frowned. "I got two, why?"

"One of 'em's still breathing, that's why!"

"How can you tell all that just by the weight of the bag?"

"It's a hobby of mine. You could put a carrier bag of assorted supermarket items on my 'ead an' I'd tell you everything that was in it, right down to the last puffin flavoured yogurt."

At that very moment his pursuers came panting over the hill, expecting to see Jim still walking some distance ahead of them. When they saw him sitting on a bench just a few yards away it was too late. Again the younger man stopped so suddenly his partner bumbled into him with a surprised gasp, and the two of them ended up in a heap on the ground.

Then they were up and running happily towards Jim like two joggers out for a bit of fresh air.

As soon as Jim saw the lip ring he was on his feet and running as well, the schoolbag containing the mobile flapping awkwardly over his shoulder like a rodeo rider, the tuna bap still in his hand.

"Come 'ere you!" shouted the younger man, who didn't seem to be gaining on him when Jim stole a quick look back. The older man was definitely falling behind, grunting like an old camel, thought Jim. Not that he'd ever seen a camel wearing a black suit. All the ones he'd seen had worn the regulation camel-hair coat.

Jim was annoyed at having to leave the rest of his

lunch on the bench. He almost considered taking a circular route that would bring him back to it, but by the time he reached the bag it would probably have been raided by seagulls and bits of Rosa's chicken curry bap and custard slice would be flying off in all directions.

Ahead of him Jim caught sight of a gate next to a National Trust sign, and beyond that a vast expanse of empty air where the coast path abruptly turned downward out of sight.

Bang! Squeeeeek-bang! went the stout wooden gate as Jim crashed through. (It was the kind that swings within its own little enclosure.)

"Young tearaway!" barked the gate. "I 'ope you sit on an ant's nest!"

Then Jim was both running and falling, pulled by gravity as the steep path became a series of wooden steps cut into the hillside, and sheep in a field on his left all turned their heads sharply together to see what the commotion was before scattering like, well, sheep.

"Ow!" "Ow!" "Ow!" "Ow!" "Ow!" "Ow!" went each of the steps in turn as Jim's feet landed heavily on them. "Ow!" "Ow!" "Ow!" "Ow!" "Ow!" "Ow!" they carried on until he'd reached the bottom.

When he turned to look back the way he'd come it was a comfortingly long while before he heard the wooden gate go Bang! Squeeeeek-bang! again, by which time he was racing towards a second gate at the opposite end of the sheep field. He could see that the path led down to the beach a very long way below. The black dots down there on the beach must be people. There was even a really tiny black dot that could have been a dog, though at this distance it could just as easily have been a miniature hippopotamus. If he could reach the beach before the men caught up, surely he'd be safe.

At the next gate he looked back to see the younger man doubled over, coughing the way smokers do when they run. (Jim's mum said running makes the soot in their lungs billow up in black clouds.) All the sheep were standing together at the far end of the field, staring at the man and laughing. The older man was nowhere in sight.

"This a paper chase then?" the old wooden gatepost said to Jim.

"What's a paper chase?" asked Jim, checking to ensure the mobile was still safe in his schoolbag.

"It's when bits of paper chase each other across fields," said the gatepost.

"No," Jim told it. "This is nothing like that. Two men are chasing me."

"Are you sure they're not paper?" asked the gatepost. "The wind can play tricks on the mind you know."

"'E's right about that," agreed the little round public footpath sign on the gatepost. "I once saw a bird with a big flat 'ead flying round in circles till it flew into an old gentleman walking his dog. Knocked 'is false teeth clean out of 'is mouth."

"Yeah, an' 'is glass eye went flyin' as well!" added one of the screws in the footpath sign.

"Then his 'ead fell off and the dog ran away with it," squeaked the old gate hinge.

"That was before his big red nose exploded and

lemonade started squirting out of his ears," chuckled a rusty nail in the gatepost.

Jim set off running down the field towards the beach.

"The bird with a big flat 'ead – "the little round sign called after Jim – "turned out to be a gull with a Rosa's bag stuck on its 'ead."

The next time he looked back, the man with the ring through his lip was sitting on the grass smoking a cigarette. He waved at Jim, which seemed an odd thing to do. Jim decided not to wave back. After all, he'd lost his chicken curry bap because of him. Instead he took out the mobile and told it what had happened.

"Let's take them on a wild goose chase," it suggested.

Jim looked doubtful. "That's when you lead someone the wrong way isn't it? But I'll probably get lost as well."

"Not if I can help it," said the mobile. "We'll follow this path all the way down, then go along the beach into Sidmouth. They'll think that's where you're staying, comprende?"

Jim could see that the black people-dots were still on the beach. The miniature hippopotamus kept running in and out of the sea.

"Comprende," said Jim, and began his descent.

The men followed, but at a leisurely pace this time.

23
I couldn't eat two.

It took Jim ten minutes to reach the beach. Surprisingly there were no people or small hippopotamuses here now. He decided it would have been a nice place to spend an afternoon if you weren't being chased. The sea made a lovely swishing sound as it swept in and out, dragging the pebbles with it.

"Eeek! What's that noise?!" shrieked the schoolbag when Jim unzipped its mouth to take out the mobile.

"You mean that swishy sound? It's only the sea."

"What's the sea?" asked the schoolbag, the bottom lip of its wide mouth trembling.

"It's what comes after A and B," said the mobile. "You should know that, being a schoolbag."

Jim noticed some bushes under the cliffs where the vegetation was really quite dense, and he had an idea.

"Listen," he said, "instead of walking all the way to Sidmouth, we could hide until those men have gone." He pointed along the beach to where the cliff protruded. "They'll think we went round that corner and follow us. Then we can just go back the way we came."

"Yes, that might work," said the mobile.

Jim immediately ran across the shingle and began searching for a good hiding place in the bushes.

A discarded flip-flop gave him a pitiful stare. "If you're planning to escape, please take me with you. I don't want to end up on a string around the neck of a cannibal!"

"Along with all those horrible shrunken monkey heads!" said an empty cigarette packet.

"Not to mention the football boots and policemen's helmets," added a Tesco carrier bag as it blew by, on its holidays from somewhere inland.

"I'm sorry but we've got to hide," said Jim, crouching down in a thick patch of bushes, and just in time for at that moment the unpleasant man with the lip ring crunched into view over the shingle, his eyes slitted against the brightness. He stopped and turned to wait for his partner, giving Jim a good view of his neat twin pony tails, one just above the other.

"There's one of them cannibals now!" called the flip-flop. "I've 'eard they do terrible things to defenceless footwear."

"Like what?" called an orange fishing buoy that lay amongst the flotsam and jetsam. "Wearing a sandal like you on one foot and knitted tea-cosy on the other, that sort of thing?"

"While pushing a dead dog in a wheelbarrow," said a no-litter sign that someone had flung from the cliff-top.

"Mock all you like," complained the flip-flop, "but

you won't be so clever when the chief cannibal has you decorating his ice-cream van!"

"I thought cannibals lived in mud huts?" said the sign.

"Not in Devon they don't," replied the flip-flop. "People would talk!"

The fishing buoy swapped a look with the no-litter sign. "I wouldn't mind living with a cannibal in an ice-cream van," it said. "We'd be well looked after with a roof over our head. Besides, I never heard of a cannibal eating a fishing buoy."

"Or a no-litter sign," added the no-litter sign confidently. "In fact the chief would probably wear me on his chest!"

"And me dangling from his backside!" said the buoy.

Jim watched the younger man trudge down to the water's edge for a better view along the beach, holding both hands to his eyes shaped into binoculars.

Then the older man appeared, wiping his face with a red spotted handkerchief as he clambered unsteadily over the shingle.

"See 'im?"

"Nah. Must've gone round the headland towards Sidcup."

"D'yer mean Sidmouth?"

"What?"

"That's Sidmouth innit? Sidcup's in Wales. Er, can I borrow your binoculars?"

"'E's not there," said the younger man impatiently.

"I want to look anyway," said the older man. He crunched over the pebbles, took the younger man's hands – still in the shape of binoculars – and held them to his own eyes."

"See anything?" asked the younger man.

"Thought I saw a big red thing bobbing up and down in the sea."

"What, like a double-decker bus you mean?"

"Post offices are red as well."

"Er, can I have my binoculars back now please?" the younger man said, snatching his hands away. "And can we stop behaving like characters in a Punch and Judy show and get after whatsisname?"

They set off in the direction of Sidmouth, their crunching footsteps echoing back from the base of the cliff.

As they passed by his hiding place, Jim heard the older man say, "Last Punch and Judy show I saw was in Southend when I were just a little kid, out for the day with me mum and dad."

"Dead now are they?" the younger man asked conversationally.

"What, me mum and dad?"

The younger man gave him a dopey look. "No, Punch and Judy."

"'Course they're not dead. They're puppets."

"Your mum and dad are puppets are they? Explains a lot that does."

"Yeah, I remember now," said the older man. "The baby fell out of the Punch and Judy box and landed on a fat lady's 'ead, an' this little dog ran off with it."

"What, the fat lady's 'ead?"

"No, the baby. 'Course it wasn't a real baby."

"Not real like Punch and Judy you mean?"

Jim couldn't hear any more of their conversation because they were well on their way to the headland.

Once they rounded the rocky outcrop, Jim could go back up the cliff path.

"That was a good idea of yours, hiding," said the mobile. "Saved us a long walk."

"Yeah, your feet must be killing you," the schoolbag told the mobile.

"No," replied the mobile, "but your mouth is proving to be a bit of a pain."

"I think I'd better put you in here..." said Jim, dropping the mobile into the bag..."and zip you up."

Before the bag could protest, Jim zipped its mouth shut. With one last look in the direction the men had gone he came out of the bushes and set off back towards the cliff path.

When he eventually reached the bench on the clifftop, he had the consolation of finding his Rosa's Bakery bag where he'd left it, with the contents still inside, waiting for him. They tasted better than he'd expected after all the excitement.

24

Oh no, not them again!

By the time Jim reached the cottage the sun was so low it made long shadows under the trees. He unlocked the front door and stepped into the living room, to be greeted by a jovial, "Ah-ha, 'oo's this then?" from the old barrel.

As he closed the door behind him, the footstool said, "It's alright boy, old George fergets everything, but we know 'oo you are. Come on in."

"'E is in," the first horse brass observed.

"So 'ow can 'e come in then?" asked the second horse brass.

"'E could go out and come in again," the brass-handled fire-iron explained.

"Ar, but what if old George said 'come in' again when 'e was already in the second time?" proposed the copper warming pan.

"Well, then 'e'd 'ave to go out and come back in a third time," said the footstool.

"'E couldn't keep doin' that," said the grandmother clock between ticks, "'e might meet 'imself comin' back the other way!"

"Even worse," said the warming pan, "'e might

meet somebody else."

"And another thing," said the grandmother clock, "if 'e kept goin' through that same bit of space 'e'd wear a hole in it."

Jim sighed tiredly. "You can't wear a hole in space. Space is just space."

"Oh-ho no it isn't," twinkled the first horse brass. "That's more townie talk. Listen, if you can't wear 'oles in space, 'ow do you account for the pebble 'ere 'aving a piece of space worn away through its middle?"

Silence weighed heavily on the air until the kettle in the hearth tinkled its lid.

"Don't take no notice of this lot, they're all mad anyway. You'll be better off gettin' them 'edge'ogs rounded up from your bedroom while it's still light. They can make one 'eck of a mess of the walls if you've left the lid off a tin of paint."

"What do you mean?" said Jim.

The warming pan made a sound like a mouse blowing it's nose in a bucket. "There's nothing 'edge'ogs enjoys more in the middle of the night, when the snow's whistling round the rooftop, than walking up the walls and across the ceiling with paint on their paws...an' if somebody 'appens to be asleep in bed... no, I can't say it. It's too awful."

"What is?" the first horse brass asked.

"Yeah, go on, tell us," encouraged the second horse brass eagerly.

"Alright then. The person in bed wakes up in the mornin', looks in the mirror and sees tiny paw prints all over their clock!"

"What?" asked the grandmother clock, shocked.

"'E means face," clarified the kettle. "Clock face. It's a figure of speech."

At this point Jim set about making another fire in the grate to warm the old place and its occupants again. That done, he stood with his back to the fire, looking forward to more of those nice sausages with the green herby bits in them. He didn't miss his mum quite so much now, but the thought of his dad still gave him an empty feeling.

As the ancient grandmother clock slowly tick-tock-twang-boinged away the time, the Toby jug said, "'Bout time for a cuppa ain't it Jim?" from its niche in the fireplace.

Jim picked up the mobile – as much from habit as anything else – and went through the tiny lobby to the equally tiny kitchen, which seemed to have grown smaller if such a thing was possible.

"I know what you want," said the miniature teapot.

"Does 'e want to be wrapped in an old carpet and rolled under the bed?" asked the washing up liquid bottle.

"Or sent to Coventry by registered post in an old army boot," said the light switch.

"'E might even prefer to be given a chicken soup bath and sent to bed early," suggested a spider wearing a party hat on the window sill.

"What 'e really wants," continued the teapot, "is to boil the kettle and I'll oblige with a nice pot of tea. You know where the tea is don't you?"

"Yes thank you," said Jim.

"'E likes 'is cups of tea, this one," the tiny teapot told the mobile as if they were old friends. "Tea wouldn't do you much good though, you bein' electrical an' that."

After making the tea, Jim took the sausages from the fridge and set about preparing a meal.

"Jim, I have good news!" said the mobile. "I've just learned that someone named Ronald Parkin works as a delivery man for a brewery in Cornwall."

"Which brewery is that then?" asked the teapot. "My old man Toby is sure to know of it. 'E used to be an ornament in the Wrong 'ouse till one of the cottage's visitors 'borrowed' 'im and brought 'im to live 'ere. That's 'ow we met. Romantic don't you think?"

"Oh yes," drawled the cold water tap, "'e lives in the other room, you live in 'ere, an' you never see each other. Dead romantic that is!"

"The brewery is called Lazonby's," the mobile told Jim.

"Lazonby's!?" piped up the little teapot. "Why, they deliver beer to the Wrong 'ouse. What a coincidence!"

"Do they really?" said the mobile, and instantly went into busy mode. Seconds later he was back. "All sorted. Lazonby's are making a delivery in two days, on Wednesday. With a bit of luck the delivery man will be Ronald Parkin."

"An 'e's from Cornwall is 'e?" asked the tiny fridge. It looked at the tiny cooker and sniffed. "Cornwall's alright I s'pose, if you've nowhere else to go. Me, I'd rather spend a week in an elephant factory, sewing their trunks on and watching those great big machines make their plastic ears."

"You can stuff your elephants," said the cooker. "I'd rather 'ave a beach holiday; trouble is with my fair skin I always end up sittin' in the 'otel room with a book."

"Reading's good for the mind," said the fridge.

"True enough," said the little cooker, "'cept I 'aven't got a mind so I can't read. You ever tried sittin' in an 'otel room with a book you can't read? It's frustratin'. You don't even know what it's about!"

"Try one of them talkin' books," the fridge suggested.

"I did," said the cooker dismally. "It wouldn't shut up all night. I didn't get a wink of sleep!"

"Cornwall's quite nice from what I've 'eard," the tiny teapot told them. "They 'ave clotted cream there same as we do. And crabs. I do like to see a well-dressed crab. Those little trousers and Jackets make 'em look so smart their own mother wouldn't recognise 'em I dare say."

The teapot brightened suddenly. "I could show you 'ow to dress a crab if you brought one in."

"I don't think I could dress one," said Jim. "Not if it was wriggling about all the time."

"Silly!" said the teapot. "You hypnotise 'em by wavin' a pork chop in front of their eyes and repeatin' over and over the words 'Pork chop by moonlight, please make me sleep tight'. Then you slip their little trousers on quick before they regains their senses."

25
Watch out for flying cows.

The next two days were uneventful. Jim stayed in the cottage and just sat around having strange conversations with the occupants. When Wednesday morning arrived he checked Lazonby's delivery time with the mobile; apparently it would be at twelve-thirty, lunchtime. As the pub was only a short stroll away they'd wait until midday, then walk down the lane and look for the delivery van.

Jim was getting excited. By eleven thirty he was practically shaking with anticipation and could wait no longer.

"I think we'll go now," he told the mobile, "in case the delivery comes early."

"Suits me," said the mobile.

"And me," said the Toby jug. "I could just do with some Lazonby's best bitter. Grand stuff that is!"

"But you can't drink beer," said Jim, wondering if he was being rude in some way.

"No, that's right," replied the jug jovially, "but I can hold a half pint for someone else sure enough."

"Ar, that takes me back," the barrel reminisced in

its hollow voice and broke into what sounded to Jim like an old sea shanty:

"Oh blow me down and shake my masts, we're bound for Valparaiso, with weevily biscuits and rum in our casks, an' I can't recall the rest-o, 'cept I think there was somethin' about a three legged octopus called Wilfred."

"Go on out with you young master," suggested the 1st horse brass, "before 'e goes off into another verse."

"Only worse," added the 2nd horse brass with a twinkle.

Jim put the mobile in his schoolbag, closed the cottage door behind him and took the track back to the lane. Today the sky was mostly grey (except for a few white bits where its underwear showed through). Beyond the hedge the cows stood so still they looked like models, so Jim stopped to see if one would move. After a while they moved forward slowly together, chewing as they walked - all except for one.

Then Jim noticed that its skin was cloth, and its legs moved like a person's. Or, to be more accurate, two people's.

"I been watchin' you watchin' them animals," said a well-weathered old road sign warning motorists that cattle used this lane.

"I think there's somebody inside that one," said Jim.

"Yes, I know," said the sign. "One of those turns up every now and then. They don't give much milk so we send them off to pantomimes."

When Jim looked again, the cloth cow's rear end sat down and one of its front legs waved at him.

"All I does is stand 'ere watchin' them cows. I can

134

tell the time of day and the day of the week by them. By the changes in these 'ere 'edgerows I know what month it is. The birds 'elp too. An' the weather. That's 'ow I know this is mid-December an' the cows will soon be flyin' off south for the winter."

"But it's April," Jim said.

The old road sign was suddenly alarmed. "Shush now. Don't let them cows 'ear you or they'll start buildin' their nests. Now good evenin' to you an' be on your way afore you starts any more trouble."

Jim continued on down the quiet lane thinking that if cows really did fly south for the winter, people on their flight path would have to carry umbrellas.

He soon found the pub, and there, parked outside it, was a big van from Lazonby's brewery. As Jim watched, a man emerged from the pub and got into the van through a wide side door. When Jim saw him his heart sank.

"It's not my dad," he told the mobile with tears in his eyes.

"Hey," said the mobile, "don't give up so easily."

But Jim wouldn't be consoled. He sat down on an old stone horse trough and began weeping silently, his shoulders jumping with each sob. When a hand touched his shoulder he looked up with tear-streaked cheeks.

"What's up, son?" The Lazonby's delivery man had come over to see what was wrong. "Which 'ouse is yours? Come on, I'll take you 'ome. No need for all this."

"It's...I thought...you...were my dad," Jim managed to explain between sobs.

"You waitin' for 'im to come 'ome, is that it?"

Eventually Jim explained that he'd come to Devon to find his dad. He took the small photo from his bag to show the delivery man, who raised his eyebrows in surprise.

"I think you've found 'im lad. Oh yes. That's my mate Ron. We do this run in turns, and today it's my turn."

Jim's heart leapt.

"I didn't know Ron 'ad a boy," the man said. "So far as I know 'e ain't even married. 'E's a dark 'orse alright is Ron. Well, well." He scratched his head and laughed out loud, and after some thought made a decision.

"Listen, seein' as 'ow you've come all this way, I reckon I should make a special delivery and take you to your dad. Don't know what his reaction will be when 'e sees you, but we'll cross that bridge when we gets there, alright?"

Jim nodded, feeling better. Neither of them noticed the large black car parked down the lane, just far enough away to be inconspicuous. In it sat the two men who were pursuing Jim. They watched as he and the delivery man crossed the road and disappeared behind the delivery van.

"Somefing's definitely goin' on 'ere," said the older man.

"You reckon?"

"Yeah. I bet there's a load of beer in the back of that van."

"What, just sloshing about?" asked the younger man.

"Nah. It'll be in somefing."

136

"Oh, you mean like short trousers?"

"They don't deliver beer in short trousers, do they?"

"In hot weather they might."

"An' that keeps the beer cool does it?"

The younger man looked heavenward. "Can you read what it says on that roadsign by the postbox?"

"Yeah. It says 'stop'."

"Will you?"

"Will I what?"

"Stop being stupid!"

"All I said was - "

He halted as the Lazonby's van pulled away suddenly and vanished behind a high wall. Then he looked at his mate. "What do we do now?"

The younger man sighed for effect. "We find a travel agent and book ourselves on the next flight to Australia, is what."

Before his colleague could ask why, he shouted: "Get after them!"

The car leapt forward, but when they rounded the high brick wall the van was nowhere to be seen. In fact it had driven into the rear yard of the pub, and was at that very moment being loaded with empty barrels for return to the brewery.

The men drove around the nearby lanes for miles looking for the disappearing van. By the time they returned to The Wrong House it was growing dark, and they were the first two customers of the evening. They ordered a tomato juice each.

"That delivery van?" the younger man said casually to the landlord.

"What? Lazonby's?"

"Yeah. Where'd it go when it left here earlier?"

"Well," said the landlord, "I s'pose 'e either drove down to Doddiscombsleigh and stopped at The Nobody, or 'e carried on straight back to the brewery."

The older of the men seemed confused. "Doddy-what?"

"Doddiscombsleigh. Other side of Exeter. Lovely little place, that."

"Doddiscombsleigh!" scoffed the younger man. "You certainly know 'ow to pick your names down 'ere!"

The older man looked at the landlord. "What's this Nobody then?"

"A pub o' course," said the landlord, "an' there's a story behind that name. See, the pub at Doddiscombsleigh is called The Nobody Inn, and one night, long ago, they 'ad burglars when the place was closed for redecoration. That was when the phone rang, and one of the burglars picked it up and said, 'There's nobody in'."

The younger man looked incredulous. "Do what?"

"It's right alright. Well, 'e could 'ardly say 'I'm not s'posed to be 'ere', now could 'e? An' that's 'ow the Nobody Inn got its name."

The two men looked at each other, then the older one burst out laughing. Presently he said, "Yeah, 's a good story that. Nobody in – Nobody Inn!"

But the younger man looked serious. "So where's this Lazonby's brewery then?"

"That be in St Austell."

"St Austell? Where's that?"

"Cornwall."

"Cornwall!?"

"S'right. You comes to it on the far side of Devon, just south of Tavistock so I'm told. I never been."

"I 'ave," piped up the older man. "When I was a kid. There was a lot of big rocks and nice beaches."

"An' I'll bet they were right next to the sea, yeah?" said the younger man sourly.

"'Ow'd you know?"

"Call it a lucky guess."

The younger man turned back to the landlord. "Er, you didn't 'appen to notice a kid 'angin' round outside earlier on?"

"You mean the boy?"

"Yeah, the boy. What was 'e doin' 'ere?"

"Don't rightly know," said the landlord. "Sat in the van while Ken loaded the empties, then off they went. I assumed 'e was Ken's nephew or somethin'. What interest is it of yours?"

"Oh, we're just nosey," said the older man.

"Really?" said the landlord. "So is there anything else you'd like to be nosey about while you're 'ere?"

"Yeah. Are you wearin' that stupid red nose for a bet, or is it Comic Relief week?"

"Don't listen to 'im," the younger man said. "See, we saw this kid cryin' 'is eyes out and we just wondered."

"Well 'e was alright when I went out the back yard to water the wife's ladybirds."

The younger man seemed annoyed. "You mean the van was in your back yard?"

"'Course. Pickin' up the empties."

At this point the older man went to see the ladybirds, and the landlord noticed their untouched drinks.

"You not goin' to drink those?"

The younger man looked serious. "Listen, if you knew 'ow many tomatoes 'ad to die to make a bottle of this stuff, you wouldn't either."

26
You winding me up?

It was half past four in the afternoon. Jim knew because Ken had left his wristwatch on the seat while he made a delivery on their way back to Cornwall. Ken had explained how he'd once accidentally cracked the glass of his watch on a barrel and didn't want to do it again.

"Hi," the watch said to Jim in a clockwise sort of way. "I don't suppose you could tell me the time."

Jim produced his customary frown. "Don't you know? You're a watch."

"Ha!" said the watch. "So you noticed. Ok, I can't deny it. I'll come clean officer. I'm a watch. I've been early, I've been late. I've done time, and so on. But I can't see myself can I? Ever thought of that? I can tell you the time, but I don't know what it is. We live in crazy times my friend."

Jim peered into the watch's face. "You're half past four and a bit."

Now it was the watch's turn to frown. "No, no, I'm not half past four and a bit. It's half past four and a bit, it being the time. I'm not the time myself, I'm merely a measurement of time. See what I'm saying?"

"Do you know my dad?" Jim asked, feeling he'd

just been ticked off.

"Who's your dad?"

"He works for the brewery."

"I might have seen him, but at the time I wouldn't have known he was your dad would I? To me he would simply have been the wrist that his watch was wearing."

Jim looked thoughtful. "Is that like a dog taking its owner for a walk?"

"What's a dog?"

"They're hairy with four legs and a tail. And they bark."

"You're winding me up! Do they wear watches?"

"Not usually."

The steering wheel turned to the beer delivery document lying on the driver's seat next to the watch. "Do you know Jim's dad by any chance?"

The document seemed uninterested in the question, being a piece of paper with no understanding of the world.

"Not me chief," it said flatly. "I only work 'ere." What little inflection it gave the words was caused by the indentations left by the biro that had written the delivery instructions.

"Ken tried to call Jim's dad on his mobile earlier," breathed the van's heater vent, "but he got no answer."

At that moment the van door opened and Ken climbed in, rubbing his back. "Those light ales never seem to get any lighter!" He laughed loudly at his own joke and they set off back to the brewery in St Austell.

They were not the only ones heading for St Austell. Ten miles away a large black car filled with cigarette smoke sped along the road north of Dartmoor towards the Cornwall county boundary. The two men planned to wait for Jim at the entrance to the brewery.

"An' then what we gonna do?" asked the older man, sucking a sweet.

The younger man gave him a tired look. "What d'you think we're gonna do, eh?"

The other man paused his sweet sucking to think. "Well, I s'pose we'll ask him some questions, and..."

"And?"

"Dunno."

"You don't know much about childcare do you? It's no good just askin' kids questions; you 'ave to use psychology."

The older man resumed his sweet sucking. "My auntie Betty used psychology on 'er parrot."

"Yeah?"

"Yeah. She'd tap the parrot on the 'ead with a banana every mornin' and say over and over again: 'Polly wants a banana, Polly wants a banana'."

"And?"

"The parrot learned to say, 'Stop 'ittin' me with that boggin' banana!'"

"So what 'appened to your auntie Betty's parrot?"

"It died on Christmas day."

"How?"

"Got drunk and fell in the deep fat fryer."

The younger man burst out laughing. "Oh, that is sad."

"Don't know why you're laughin'. It was a nice little parrot."

A few miles further on the older man said, "My auntie Betty snuffed it soon after the parrot."

"Not the deep fat fryer?"
"Nah. Moths."

27

The Owl's Earmuffs.

Two hours later they parked in St Austell High Street opposite Lazonby's brewery.

"So what's next?" asked the older man, aware of the emptiness in his stomach. There was a Chinese take-away just a bit further up the road.

"I can't tell you that," answered the younger man melodramatically. "You might be captured by the enemy and forced to reveal our plans. And where would we be then, eh?"

"The enemy? A kid?"

"An how d'you know he's not a shape-shifting alien from another world pretending to be a kid?"

"A wot!?"

"You know, like that blue kid in the X-men? See, there's a lot of things you don't know about this situation, and what you don't know could be dangerous."

The older man gazed longingly at the Chinese take-away sign and heard his stomach gurgle.

At that exact same moment the Lazonby's van was twelve miles away on the St Austell road.

"Where are we?" Jim asked, staring out at the road coming towards them in the van's headlights.

"On a dark night like this we could be almost anywhere," drawled the van's heater vent. "Time plays tricks here on Dartmoor and things are never what they seem."

"That's right," confirmed the door handle. "Entire villages have been known to vanish, their inhabitants never seen again."

"The milk can turn to jelly before your eyes, and cucumbers can fly," added the handbrake.

"According to my mapping," the mobile whispered to Jim, "the A393 goes off to the right and would take us to Redruth, while a left turn would take us to Penryn."

"Coo, your old mobile's a bit sharp aint 'e?" observed the steering wheel in Ken's hands.

"Ken usually forgets to switch 'is mobile on," said the heater vent. "'Gets 'im in trouble with the brewery it do."

"Forgot 'is trousers one mornin'," said the gear knob.

"Even 'ad 'is boots on the wrong feet another time," said the door handle.

The biro poked its tiny head from Jim's schoolbag. "Who's feet did he have them on?"

"No idea," said the door handle. "It were a total stranger."

Jim looked at Ken. "Is your mobile switched on?"

"What? Eh?" said Ken, as if woken from a light sleep. "Me mobile? Why?"

"In case the brewery need to talk to you."

At that, Ken began rummaging in the door pocket for his mobile, except it wasn't in there.

"Now where did I...?"

"Ask 'im if 'e's looked on 'is belt where 'e usually keeps it," suggested the steering wheel.

"It's there alright," rasped the heater vent. "I can see it!"

"Tell 'im then, in case we 'ave to change our route like we did that time it snowed, remember?"

"Brrr, don't remind me!" said the plastic dolphin dangling from the rear-view mirror, shivering on its string at the memory.

"Middle of winter it was," the steering wheel explained to Jim while Ken continued feeling around the cab for his mobile. "Snow 'undreds of miles deep - like the top of a giant trifle it was – an' cold as a penguin's toenails. There we were, lookin' for a pub!"

"To make a delivery see," clarified the floor mat.

"Which pub was it?" inquired the gear lever knob.

"I think it were The Leg of Old White Horse with a Side Order of Egg and Chips," said the heater vent.

"No," corrected the steering wheel roundly, "that's over St. Ives way. It must've been The Owl's Earmuffs up by Grimspound."

"Or The Three Flyin' Cucumbers," suggested the dolphin.

"An' we got stuck in a drift by that old stone bridge," the heater vent reminisced. "That was when Ken got out to shovel snow and we saw the ghost of the old 'angman's carpet slippers."

"Yeah," added the gear knob excitedly, "an' a herd of really tiny mammoths!"

"They weren't mammoths, they were Dartmoor ponies," the steering wheel corrected him, "covered in snow."

"Ken? Your mobile." Jim tried again.

"What?"

"Your mobile - it's fastened to your belt."

"Me belt - ?" Ken looked down, causing him to miss the turning to Falmouth. Instead the delivery van sped through an open gate, bounced down a grassy slope and ended up in a duck pond, whereupon the empty beer barrels began floating out of the back of the van to sit bobbing in the dark water.

"I knew that was a bad idea," said Jim's mobile. "Ken needs all his concentration for driving."

"An' a bit more besides," added the steering wheel. "He really should keep his eyes open."

"And his nose shut," said the gear knob.

"And his bicycle under his bed in case there's a flood in the night," whispered Jim's schoolbag.

"His bicycle?" said Jim.

"'E means 'is lifejacket," said the gearknob.

"No I don't," said the schoolbag. "I mean one of those inflatable bikes with a transmitter and a supply of drinking-water, in case he's not picked up for days."

"Imagine that," said the biro in Jim's bag, shivering. "I once knew a felt-tip pen who wasn't picked up for months. Completely dried it did, end of story. But that's not going to happen to me. I'll die writing!"

28
Well I Never!

It took Ken over an hour to round up the barrels and back the van out of the pond and up the slope to the road. By that time, miles away, the brewery had closed its doors for the night, and as the Lazonby's van still hadn't turned up, the two men decided they ought to find the hotel they'd booked. But first, as the pub opposite the brewery was still open, they'd sample a pint or two of Lazonby's beer to wash down the Chinese take-away they'd just eaten in the car.

They had no idea that hidden away down a narrow lane just a mile or so away was a row of tiny terraced cottages. Once occupied by members of the Coast Guard, the cottages were now sometimes rented out to holidaymakers.

While the men enjoyed their beer, two headlights appeared in the darkness at the top of the lane and followed it down to the last cottage, nearest to the sea. There the van stopped and Ken turned off the engine.

"Well matey, this is where your dad lives."

Jim was too excited to speak and just sat there staring at the two small lighted windows across the lane, his eyes big and round as moons.

"Come on," said Ken, understanding a little of Jim's concern. "I'll take you in and, er, kind of introduce you if you like."

Together they crossed the narrow lane, able to smell the sea and hear the waves breaking on the rocks just a bit further on.

Ken gave a firm knock on the cottage door and opened it, stuck his head inside and called: "Ahoy there shipmate. You at home? It's Ken."

"We're closed. Come back tomorrow," Jim heard an unfamiliar voice answer.

Ken sniggered for Jim's benefit. "That's Ron for you. Always ready with a joke."

"An' 'is trousers rolled up to 'is elbows," commented the bootscraper by the door.

Ken called back: "Ron, I brought somebody to see you."

The tone of Ron's voice had changed when he called back. "Oh yeah? You know I don't like surprises."

Then Ron himself appeared. "Who's this then?" he said, frowning at Jim, who frowned back.

"Well I never," said Ken. "You two don't arf look like each other, but I s'pose that's only natural, you bein', er..."

At that, Ron's eyebrows twitched upward and his frown disappeared. He examined Jim's face with a mixture of wonder and confusion. "Jim!" was all he could say, as if he'd just learned a new word. "Jim."

This was not how Jim had expected it to be. He felt none of the emotion he'd experienced earlier; there were no tears, no memories flooding back. He felt simply that his mission was accomplished.

150

After a few seconds' silence Ken said, "Well, I, er, better be off then. 'S'pect you two 'ave a lot to talk about. I got to take the van back any'ow."

As Jim and his dad watched the van drive away up the lane, Ron said, "Well Jim, just you and me now. You want to come in have a drink and a bite to eat?"

"Tea," said Jim in a tiny voice.

"What?"

"I like tea."

They went in and closed the door. Ron made the tea, then joined Jim in the living room where they sat together by the fire while Jim explained about the two men coming to the house, threatening his mum and Lucinda. He talked about finding the bank book, described his trip to Devon, the rented cottage, and being followed to Sidmouth by the men.

When he'd finished, his dad sat back in his old armchair and appeared deep in thought. At length he leaned forward and put a hand on Jim's shoulder.

"Alright matey, I suppose I may as well come clean and tell you the truth." And he proceeded to explain how he'd become involved with a criminal gang in a robbery; how he'd been employed by them to drive the getaway car, and how something had gone wrong during the robbery so he'd been forced to drive off alone with half a million pounds of stolen cash. If he hadn't, he'd have been caught along with the rest of the gang.

"Naturally they assumed I'd deliberately run off with all the money," said Jim's dad, "so when they got out of prison, they came looking for me. At the time I really didn't know what to do for the best so I arranged for the money to find its way into that mysterious account of yours, and I tried to forget about the whole thing."

"So what are you going to do?" asked Jim.

"You mean what are we going to do, don't you? We're in this together now. Those men were probably hoping you'd lead them to me."

He smiled, but it was not a happy smile. "See Jim, one reason I went into hiding after the robbery was to protect you and your mum. I figured that with me gone, those men would leave you in peace. I thought it had worked too until you showed up here."

Jim looked into the fire. "I didn't mean to get you into trouble...dad." A tear ran down his face.

"Aw, hey, come on mate. You didn't get me in trouble – it was the other way around!" He put an arm round Jim's shoulders, and together they watched flames dance in the fireplace.

29

Three 'undred fathoms.

A bit later Jim's dad made up a bed for him in the living room beside the fire. The cottage had two bedrooms, but as there was no heating in them, they decided Jim would be better off here.

When his dad had gone up to bed, Jim lay tucked up on a mattress watching the shadows cast on the low ceiling by the fire's last few flames. Then he remembered the mobile and reached for his schoolbag.

"Ah, there you are," said the mobile, "but where is this?"

"It's my dad's house."

On the small hearth a large brown pebble eyed the mobile. "A talking phone?" it said. "That's interesting. I've seen a phone you talk to, but not one that speaks for itself."

"And you find that unusual do you?" asked the mobile. "More unusual than a pebble giving voice to its opinions?"

"Pardon us for being here," muttered the piece of

driftwood beside the pebble.

The mobile turned to Jim. "You should have introduced me to your dad so we could renew our acquaintance."

Jim looked uncomfortable. "Sorry. I just forgot. There's been so much happening."

"Hey, give the kid a break!" said the red and green sailboat on the mantelpiece. "'E's not seen 'is dad for...'ow long was it?"

"Three 'undred fathoms," rasped the box of sailor's knots on the wall.

"Three 'undred fathoms? Is that a long time?" the sailboat looked to the knots for confirmation.

"It's exactly ten minutes an' a bit."

The mobile snorted at their ignorance. "You lot are on another planet."

"A planet?" inquired the driftwood. "What's one of those?"

A large pink sea shell in the hearth sniffed to clear its cavities. "Well," it said, "I'm no expert, but by my reckoning, if a little pig is a piglet, and a little whip is a whippet, then a planet is a little plan."

"I always thought a little pig was a pigling," said the box of knots. "And what about a little whistle? Surely that's a whistling?"

"Right," the pebble joined in, "and that makes a little tick a tickling."

"I beg to differ," differed the sea shell hollowly, "but a little tick is a ticket."

"An' I s'pose a small rock is a rocket," said the pebble, "a small lock a locket, an' a diminutive midge a midget?"

154

Jim rubbed his eyes and yawned. "I really do want to go to sleep now," he told no one in particular. Then to the mobile said, "Can you wait till tomorrow to hear the latest news?"

"That's no good," said the sailboat. "By the time tomorrow gets 'ere, it'll be today an' we'll 'ave missed it."

"An' today will be yesterday," said the driftwood, "so we'll 'ave missed that as well!"

At that, Jim turned off the mobile and tried to get some sleep.

When he awoke the fire was almost out. He felt cold and thirsty, and was trying to remember the conversation with his dad when something scraped along the window. When the sound came again it was more of a metallic tinkle – as if the window catch had just been disengaged and someone was trying to get in!

Then the curtain rustled and Jim's heart missed a beat because someone was climbing through the open window; he could see a leg with a shoe on the end.

He couldn't simply sit there and do nothing, especially now that someone was whispering, and being answered by another whisper. Even in whispers he recognised the two voices. He could see their faces in his mind, one stupid, the other smiling wickedly, the tiny ring gleaming in his lip.

In a flash Jim was in his shoes and running up the creaky wooden stairs with his schoolbag slung over his shoulder to find his dad waiting for him.

"Dad - !"

"I know," his dad said in a hushed voice. "Come on."

In the tiny bedroom Jim's dad opened the window, and as they climbed down onto the roof of a small shed Jim could hear noises coming from the open window above: bangs, the crashing of furniture, a series of piercing squeaks that could well have been aardvarks singing, followed by someone blowing a tremendously loud raspberry - or had he only imagined that?

Once they were on the ground, Jim and his dad raced through the garden and soon emerged onto the coast path that snaked along the top of the cliffs. Jim's dad seemed to know the way, which was just as well because, unbeknown to Jim, the side of the cliff had fallen away in places and taken the path with it, depositing great piles of earth and rock on the beach far below. Anyone not watching their step could easily fall to their doom!

As they raced along it was too dark to see for more than a few steps ahead, yet Jim could hear the waves crashing against the rocks in the darkness.

When his dad came to a sudden halt they stood and listened out for their pursuers. That was when a sharp 'CRACK' split the darkness, and Jim felt his dad fall to the ground.

The men had a gun! His dad had been hit by a 'shot in the dark'.

Now Jim heard the pounding of running feet, and just when it seemed certain they would be captured, a hand grabbed his arm and he was pulled sideways into darkness and empty space...

A moment later he landed with a branch-snapping crash in what felt like dense bushes, but gravity wasn't done with him yet. He bounced like a ball and went rolling over and over down a steep grassy slope while sharp thorns caught at his clothes and bit at his hands and face, and he imagined himself falling to the unseen rocks far below.

Then everything went black.

30
He broke a leg.

When he woke up Jim recognised the special smell that hospitals have, and someone was saying his name over and over: Jim? Jim? Jim?

Jim opened his eyes to find his mum bending over him, making a clown face by crying and trying to smile both together. Just behind her, Lucinda was wearing exactly the same face. So were each of Lucinda's big bobbly earrings.

A doctor in a white coat appeared beside them. The stethoscope around his neck tut-tutted at Jim.

"My diagnosis is that you fell off a cliff backwards," said the stethoscope.

"How do Jim?" said the doctor, checking the progress report in his hand. "Well now, apart from a few scratches and scrapes you'll be good to go in a day or so."

"And great news," said the pen in the doctor's pocket, "they're sending you to the home for lost dogs!"

"And chickens with wooden legs," croaked the switch on the bedside light.

"Because they've been cheeky to bus drivers," whispered one of the grapes Jim's mum had brought.

"And then you'll be forced to take all the dogs and chickens for walks and make little saddles for them and buy them jelly babies!" added one of Lucinda's bobbly earrings with a smirk.

Jim rubbed his eyes and tried to sit up in the hospital bed, but everything ached so much he just grimaced and lay back again. Even the bed seemed to ache.

"What happened to my dad? Is he alright? Those men shot him!"

"Now don't you worry about your dad," the doctor said. "The wound was pretty superficial, lucky for him. He wasn't quite so lucky with the fall. Broke a leg – one of his own as it happens - and fractured his wrist, but he's fine otherwise. I reckon the both of you got off lightly considering."

"That's right," said the handle on the bedside table, "considering you could've been swallowed by a giant tortoise."

"Or dragged off by wild toothbrushes," added the switch on the bedside light. "This is Cornwall after all."

Then his mum was all over Jim, hugging and kissing him and wetting his face with salty tears.

It was more than the apple on Jim's bedside table could bear to watch. "Yuk!" was all it said.

And there was more unhappy news: While Jim had been lucky to have fallen off the cliff just where he did – and finished up on a ledge half way down - his schoolbag had fared less well and crashed onto the rocks below. A short while later someone recovered it, and inside found the old mobile, shattered into useless fragments.

A few days later they allowed Jim to go home with his mum and Lucinda, who had both stayed in a nearby hotel waiting for him to recover. But of course that wasn't the end of the story by any means – there was still the business of the stolen money.

A police inspector came to the house specially to see Jim about that. There was a reward for the return of the £500,000, and they decided Jim should have that. After all, he'd been responsible for the capture of the criminals, the police inspector told him.

They'd overlook the fact that Jim had spent some of the money on his trip to Devon, including his rail fare and the rent of a cottage - not to mention the small matter of some rather expensive sausages.

"Smart of you to use that old mobile and keep us posted on your location," the police Inspector told him, "and to send us constant updates of the situation."

Of course Jim could hardly explain that the mobile had done all that by itself.

"We were able to follow you all the way. Led us straight to the spot on the cliff where you fell over the edge."

At that point Jim's mum had to go and find a tissue to blow her nose and mop her eyes again. Even Lucinda came in specially to give Jim a kiss on the cheek. (Jim's mum had bribed her to do it, but she spoiled it by poking her tongue out at Jim as a departing gesture. So did her bobbly earrings.)

"I expect you'll want to know what's going to happen to your dad?" said the police Inspector while Jim's mum was in the kitchen making more tea.

Jim said nothing, afraid it would be bad news.

A shortbread biscuit on the plate Jim's mum had brought in shook its head. "I expect they'll turn 'im into teacakes," it said to the bun next to it, "with currants in 'em."

"Could be worse," said the bun.

"Yeah, but these are electric currants!"

"N-i-c-e," said the bun slowly, savouring the thought.

In fact there was no bad news. Not really. It turned out the police knew all about the bungled robbery of a few years earlier; they knew about Jim's dad's role as a getaway driver. He was never a proper member of the criminal gang, just someone who'd made a wrong decision and found himself carried along by events beyond his control.

Though Jim didn't understand the legal details, it transpired that his dad would probably receive a suspended prison sentence and be put on probation. At least it meant he wouldn't have to go to prison.

The very best part of all, so far as Jim was concerned, was that his dad had decided to leave Cornwall and come to live nearby.

31

Voices have no sense of direction.

Not long after Jim received that piece of news, the postman brought him a package; inside was a note from his dad, together with a shiny new smartphone complete with its own charger. The note said a SIM card would follow in the post so Jim could use his new phone to connect to the internet and do all kinds of other things too. Yet though the smartphone was one of the latest kind, it couldn't make up for the loss of his dad's old mobile.

That evening Jim sat on his bed trying to understand the instructions in the smartphone's manual.

"Er...where's your old mobile, Jim?" inquired the pterodactyl from overhead.

"Is it still on holiday in Cornwall?" the marble asked in its squeaky little voice.

"I hope it sends us a nice postcard," said Mister Potato Head.

"My dad's old mobile doesn't work any more," he told them. "When some men shot my dad I fell over a cliff, and the mobile got smashed to bits on the rocks."

He emptied the contents of his schoolbag onto the

bed to show them the mobile's remains.

"Is that all there is left of his dad?" asked the shocked potato.

"He must have been really little," squeaked the marble.

"And made of plastic and bits of wire," added the robot.

"You should have got one of those rubber dads," suggested a smelly trainer, "then it would have bounced."

Jim eyed the remains of the mobile; among them was the SIM card that had come out when the mobile landed on the rocks. He picked it up and examined it, still not sure what a SIM card did. It seemed to be quite important though.

Then he had an idea: Perhaps the old mobile's SIM would work in his new smartphone.

Using the manual as a guide, Jim managed to remove the new mobile's back cover and insert the SIM. When he'd replaced the cover he followed more instructions and switched the mobile on.

Nothing happened, which made him wonder if the SIM had been damaged in the fall. Or perhaps it was simply the wrong kind of SIM for his new phone.

"Hello?" Jim said to the mobile. "Are you working?"

There was no response.

"Would it like a sweetie?" wondered the paper clip.

"Try it with piece of cheese and a biscuit," suggested the pterodactyl.

"Tickle its turnips," offered the tiny Frankenstein's monster.

"Has the cat got its tongue?" asked the robot.

"Perhaps a chicken ran off with its football boots!" squeaked the marble.

"It could simply have lost its voice," suggested a smelly trainer.

"Where?" said the potato.

"In the post," said Rupert the shark.

"Actually," said the plug on the lava lamp, "voices have no sense of direction. Without a satnav they can easily lose their way between your mouth and your ears. Mine once got stuck up my nose!"

Jim put the new smartphone on his bedside table next to Mister Potato Head and started getting ready for bed.

The potato eyed the smartphone. "Greetings," it said, "and welcome to bedside table land. Um...do you speak my language?"

The phone was silent.

"P'raps it doesn't want to be seen talking to a vegetable," ventured Rupert the shark. "You're not rich or famous, you don't have any friends on Potatobook, and you've never met the Queen's washing machine. You don't have much going for you."

"What can I do?" whimpered the potato.

"Well now," said Rupert, "if you were to make yourself into a nice plate of mash with a sausage stuck in it, even I might fancy you."

Jim climbed into bed and lay there thinking about his dad's old mobile, remembering their conversations and the adventures they'd shared. It was only with its help that he'd been reunited with his dad, and now it had gone something important was missing from his life. He'd lost a friend; perhaps the only real friend he'd ever had.

He didn't want to think any more about that and turned on his side so he could look at the objects on his bedside table.

The fat red blobs in the lava lamp went slowly up, and just as slowly down. The little marble twinkled and looked back at him like someone's glass eye. The robot's silvery body gleamed with a reddy sheen in contrast with the rough and wrinkled skin of the potato, just one of who's overlarge plastic eyes observed Jim from the middle of its brown belly.

And there, in the centre of this group, was the shiny new smartphone.

Jim suddenly remembered it still had the old mobile's SIM in it, but then decided that as it didn't work, he might as well leave it in there until the new SIM arrived.

"Goodnight," he said, and reached over to switch off the lamp as a chorus of voices came out of the darkness to wish him goodnight. He closed his eyes and tried to sleep, but there was so much spinning around inside his head that he thought he'd never drop off...

The next thing that Jim saw was a glowing figure floating in the darkness above his bed. It was Mister Potato Head wearing a ballgown covered in sparkly sequins and coloured jewels. On his head sat a silvery crown, and in his hand was a wand with a star on the end. A solitary eye gazed from his belly button. He was also wearing luminous pink lipstick which just didn't look right at all on a potato.

"I am your fairy spudmother," said the potato, "and I'm here to grant you a lucky fish."

"You mean a lucky wish don't you?" said Jim dreamily.

"Ooh, er, yes," said the potato. "Sorry. I am here to grant you a lucky wish."

The potato waved his wand at Jim's new smartphone, causing a dazzling shower of tiny bright stars to twinkle all around it.

At once the smartphone's screen came alight. It sat up and buzzed at him.

"Jim, Jim – wake up!" said a voice that Jim thought he'd never hear again.

Jim was instantly awake. He sat bolt upright in bed and switched on the lava lamp, revealing the little marble, the potato – minus ballgown, lipstick and wand - and the robot, all staring in astonishment at his new smartphone.

"Hi," said the smartphone in the familiar voice of his dad's old mobile. "Remember me?"

Jim blinked, hardly daring to believe this was happening. Could he still be asleep and dreaming?

"Don't worry," said the smartphone, "it really is me, and hey! I love this smart new body you've got for me!"

Jim was beaming with delight. "But how did you...I mean...?"

"It's a bit complicated," said the smartphone. "Let's just say it's lucky you kept my old SIM - it allowed me to find my way back here. But now I am here I've discovered that I no longer need a SIM; what's more I can do some really interesting new things..."

Without warning a ghostly image began growing out of the smartphone's screen in a solid beam of light which, miraculously, shaped itself into a three dimensional picture of Jim's dad!

The little marble squeaked with fright, the robot popped a rivet, and the potato covered its one remaining eye with both its hands.

"It's called a hologram," explained the smartphone. "It's a bit like a TV picture in three dimensions."

Jim couldn't believe his eyes.

"I can show you pictures like this of anything from my memory," said the smartphone. "And if you think that's neat, just watch this..."

The image of Jim's dad withdrew into the smartphone which then began to glow with a pale blue light. As Jim watched, wide-eyed, the smartphone rose up into the air until it hovered a few inches above the bedside table.

All of this was too much for the little marble, who hid behind the robot, who was already hiding behind Mister Potato Head.

"Now," said the smartphone, "if you wouldn't mind, Jim, I could use a charge up, but you won't need a charger – I can do it myself, wirelessly. Then we'll see how much fun we can have with all these amazing new apps..."

Proof

Made in the USA
Charleston, SC
23 January 2016